Hybrid Solutions
Complete Self-Assessment Guide

The guidance in this Self-Assessment is based on Hybrid Solutions best practices and standards in business process architecture, design and quality management. The guidance is also based on the professional judgment of the individual collaborators listed in the Acknowledgments.

Notice of rights

Trademarks

Table of Contents

About The Art of Service

The Art of Service, Business Process Architects since 2000, is dedicated to helping stakeholders achieve excellence.

Defining, designing, creating, and implementing a process to solve a stakeholders challenge or meet an objective is the most valuable role… In EVERY group, company, organization and department.

Unless you're talking a one-time, single-use project, there should be a process. Whether that process is managed and implemented by humans, AI, or a combination of the two, it needs to be designed by someone with a complex enough perspective to ask the right questions.

Someone capable of asking the right questions and step back and say, 'What are we really trying to accomplish here? And is there a different way to look at it?'

With The Art of Service's Standard Requirements Self-Assessments, we empower people who can do just that — whether their title is marketer, entrepreneur, manager, salesperson, consultant, Business Process Manager, executive assistant, IT Manager, CIO etc... —they are the people who rule the future. They are people who watch the process as it happens, and ask the right questions to make the process work better.

Contact us when you need any support with this Self-Assessment and any help with templates, blue-prints and examples of standard documents you might need:

http://theartofservice.com
service@theartofservice.com

Included Resources - how to access

Included with your purchase of the book is the Hybrid Solutions

Self-Assessment Spreadsheet Dashboard which contains all questions and Self-Assessment areas and auto-generates insights, graphs, and project RACI planning - all with examples to get you started right away.

How? Simply send an email to
access@theartofservice.com
with this books' title in the subject to get the Hybrid Solutions Self Assessment Tool right away.

You will receive the following contents with New and Updated specific criteria:

- The latest quick edition of the book in PDF

- The latest complete edition of the book in PDF, which criteria correspond to the criteria in...

- The Self-Assessment Excel Dashboard, and...

- Example pre-filled Self-Assessment Excel Dashboard to get familiar with results generation

- In-depth specific Checklists covering the topic

- Project management checklists and templates to assist with implementation

INCLUDES LIFETIME SELF ASSESSMENT UPDATES

Every self assessment comes with Lifetime Updates and Lifetime Free Updated Books. Lifetime Updates is an industry-first feature which allows you to receive verified self assessment updates, ensuring you always have the most accurate information at your fingertips.

Get it now- you will be glad you did - do it now, before you forget.

Send an email to **access@theartofservice.com** with this books' title in the subject to get the Hybrid Solutions Self Assessment Tool right away.

Purpose of this Self-Assessment

This Self-Assessment has been developed to improve understanding of the requirements and elements of Hybrid Solutions, based on best practices and standards in business process architecture, design and quality management.

It is designed to allow for a rapid Self-Assessment to determine how closely existing management practices and procedures correspond to the elements of the Self-Assessment.

The criteria of requirements and elements of Hybrid Solutions have been rephrased in the format of a Self-Assessment questionnaire, with a seven-criterion scoring system, as explained in this document.

In this format, even with limited background knowledge of Hybrid Solutions, a manager can quickly review existing operations to determine how they measure up to the standards. This in turn can serve as the starting point of a 'gap analysis' to identify management tools or system elements that might usefully be implemented in the organization to help improve overall performance.

How to use the Self-Assessment

On the following pages are a series of questions to identify to what extent your Hybrid Solutions initiative is complete in comparison to the requirements set in standards.

To facilitate answering the questions, there is a space in front of each question to enter a score on a scale of '1' to '5'.

1 Strongly Disagree

2 Disagree

3 Neutral

4 Agree

5 Strongly Agree

Read the question and rate it with the following in front of mind:

'In my belief,
the answer to this question is clearly defined'.

There are two ways in which you can choose to interpret this statement;
1. how aware are you that the answer to the question is clearly defined
2. for more in-depth analysis you can choose to gather evidence and confirm the answer to the question. This obviously will take more time, most Self-Assessment users opt for the first way to interpret the question and dig deeper later on based on the outcome of the overall Self-Assessment.

A score of '1' would mean that the answer is not clear at all, where a '5' would mean the answer is crystal clear and defined. Leave emtpy when the question is not applicable or you don't want to answer it, you can skip it without affecting your score. Write your score in the space provided.

After you have responded to all the appropriate statements in each section, compute your average score for that section, using the formula provided, and round to the nearest tenth. Then transfer to the corresponding spoke in the Hybrid Solutions Scorecard on the second next page of the Self-Assessment.

Your completed Hybrid Solutions Scorecard will give you a clear presentation of which Hybrid Solutions areas need attention.

Hybrid Solutions Scorecard Example

Example of how the finalized Scorecard can look like:

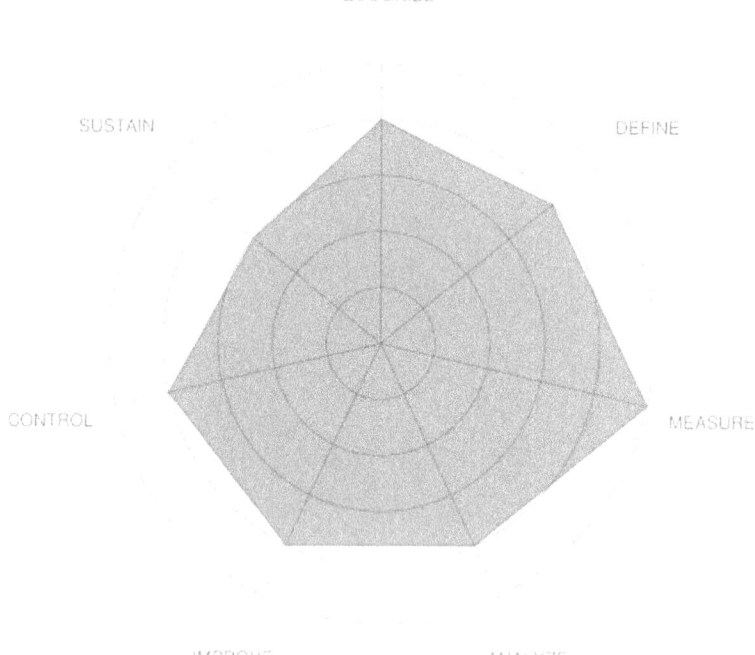

Hybrid Solutions Scorecard

Your Scores:

RECOGNIZE

SUSTAIN

DEFINE

CONTROL

MEASURE

IMPROVE

ANALYZE

BEGINNING OF THE SELF-ASSESSMENT:

CRITERION #1: RECOGNIZE

INTENT: Be aware of the need for change. Recognize that there is an unfavorable variation, problem or symptom.

In my belief, the answer to this question is clearly defined:

5 Strongly Agree

4 Agree

3 Neutral

2 Disagree

1 Strongly Disagree

1. What tools and technologies are needed for a custom Hybrid Solutions project?
<--- Score

2. What is the problem and/or vulnerability?
<--- Score

3. How do you recognize an Hybrid Solutions objection?

<--- Score

4. Is the quality assurance team identified?
<--- Score

5. What vendors make products that address the Hybrid Solutions needs?
<--- Score

6. Who needs what information?
<--- Score

7. What creative shifts do you need to take?
<--- Score

8. Are there regulatory / compliance issues?
<--- Score

9. What else needs to be measured?
<--- Score

10. What Hybrid Solutions capabilities do you need?
<--- Score

11. Are your goals realistic? Do you need to redefine your problem? Perhaps the problem has changed or maybe you have reached your goal and need to set a new one?
<--- Score

12. Will it solve real problems?
<--- Score

13. How are you going to measure success?
<--- Score

14. How do you assess your Hybrid Solutions workforce capability and capacity needs, including skills, competencies, and staffing levels?
<--- Score

15. Are there any specific expectations or concerns about the Hybrid Solutions team, Hybrid Solutions itself?
<--- Score

16. Are there any revenue recognition issues?
<--- Score

17. What are your needs in relation to Hybrid Solutions skills, labor, equipment, and markets?
<--- Score

18. Who defines the rules in relation to any given issue?
<--- Score

19. What are the clients issues and concerns?
<--- Score

20. Do you recognize Hybrid Solutions achievements?
<--- Score

21. What Hybrid Solutions problem should be solved?
<--- Score

22. Would you recognize a threat from the inside?
<--- Score

23. Is the need for organizational change recognized?

<--- Score

24. How does it fit into your organizational needs and tasks?
<--- Score

25. Who needs to know?
<--- Score

26. Do you need to avoid or amend any Hybrid Solutions activities?
<--- Score

27. How do you recognize an objection?
<--- Score

28. Whom do you really need or want to serve?
<--- Score

29. What problems are you facing and how do you consider Hybrid Solutions will circumvent those obstacles?
<--- Score

30. Are controls defined to recognize and contain problems?
<--- Score

31. Which needs are not included or involved?
<--- Score

32. Is it clear when you think of the day ahead of you what activities and tasks you need to complete?
<--- Score

33. How do you identify subcontractor relationships?
<--- Score

34. Where do you need to exercise leadership?
<--- Score

35. Are there Hybrid Solutions problems defined?
<--- Score

36. Are there recognized Hybrid Solutions problems?
<--- Score

37. What is the smallest subset of the problem you can usefully solve?
<--- Score

38. Does your organization need more Hybrid Solutions education?
<--- Score

39. What are the minority interests and what amount of minority interests can be recognized?
<--- Score

40. How can auditing be a preventative security measure?
<--- Score

41. What extra resources will you need?
<--- Score

42. Will a response program recognize when a crisis occurs and provide some level of response?
<--- Score

43. What is the extent or complexity of the Hybrid Solutions problem?

<--- Score

44. What needs to be done?

<--- Score

45. Have you identified your Hybrid Solutions key performance indicators?

<--- Score

46. Does the problem have ethical dimensions?

<--- Score

47. How much are sponsors, customers, partners, stakeholders involved in Hybrid Solutions? In other words, what are the risks, if Hybrid Solutions does not deliver successfully?

<--- Score

48. What is the recognized need?

<--- Score

49. Do you know what you need to know about Hybrid Solutions?

<--- Score

50. What training and capacity building actions are needed to implement proposed reforms?

<--- Score

51. Are losses recognized in a timely manner?

<--- Score

52. How many trainings, in total, are needed?

<--- Score

53. What does Hybrid Solutions success mean to the stakeholders?
<--- Score

54. Who should resolve the Hybrid Solutions issues?
<--- Score

55. Who needs to know about Hybrid Solutions?
<--- Score

56. Are you dealing with any of the same issues today as yesterday? What can you do about this?
<--- Score

57. Does Hybrid Solutions create potential expectations in other areas that need to be recognized and considered?
<--- Score

58. What prevents you from making the changes you know will make you a more effective Hybrid Solutions leader?
<--- Score

59. What situation(s) led to this Hybrid Solutions Self Assessment?
<--- Score

60. What do you need to start doing?
<--- Score

61. Did you miss any major Hybrid Solutions issues?
<--- Score

62. What is the problem or issue?

<--- Score

63. What Hybrid Solutions events should you attend?
<--- Score

64. What do employees need in the short term?
<--- Score

65. How do you identify the kinds of information that you will need?
<--- Score

66. To what extent would your organization benefit from being recognized as a award recipient?
<--- Score

67. What are the expected benefits of Hybrid Solutions to the stakeholder?
<--- Score

68. What information do users need?
<--- Score

69. Do you need different information or graphics?
<--- Score

70. What activities does the governance board need to consider?
<--- Score

71. What Hybrid Solutions coordination do you need?
<--- Score

72. Do you have/need 24-hour access to key personnel?

<--- Score

73. Think about the people you identified for your Hybrid Solutions project and the project responsibilities you would assign to them, what kind of training do you think they would need to perform these responsibilities effectively?
<--- Score

74. How do you take a forward-looking perspective in identifying Hybrid Solutions research related to market response and models?
<--- Score

75. Where is training needed?
<--- Score

76. Are employees recognized for desired behaviors?
<--- Score

77. Why is this needed?
<--- Score

78. Who are your key stakeholders who need to sign off?
<--- Score

79. Which issues are too important to ignore?
<--- Score

80. Looking at each person individually – does every one have the qualities which are needed to work in this group?
<--- Score

81. As a sponsor, customer or management, how important is it to meet goals, objectives?
<--- Score

82. For your Hybrid Solutions project, identify and describe the business environment, is there more than one layer to the business environment?
<--- Score

83. What are the Hybrid Solutions resources needed?
<--- Score

84. Will new equipment/products be required to facilitate Hybrid Solutions delivery, for example is new software needed?
<--- Score

85. Is it needed?
<--- Score

86. Who needs budgets?
<--- Score

87. What needs to stay?
<--- Score

88. What is the Hybrid Solutions problem definition? What do you need to resolve?
<--- Score

89. How are the Hybrid Solutions's objectives aligned to the group's overall stakeholder strategy?
<--- Score

90. Are employees recognized or rewarded for performance that demonstrates the highest levels

of integrity?
<--- Score

91. What would happen if Hybrid Solutions weren't done?
<--- Score

92. To what extent does each concerned units management team recognize Hybrid Solutions as an effective investment?
<--- Score

93. How are training requirements identified?
<--- Score

94. Why the need?
<--- Score

95. What are the stakeholder objectives to be achieved with Hybrid Solutions?
<--- Score

96. What are the timeframes required to resolve each of the issues/problems?
<--- Score

97. What resources or support might you need?
<--- Score

98. Will Hybrid Solutions deliverables need to be tested and, if so, by whom?
<--- Score

99. Who else hopes to benefit from it?
<--- Score

100. Can management personnel recognize the monetary benefit of Hybrid Solutions?
<--- Score

Add up total points for this section:
_ _ _ _ _ = Total points for this section

Divided by: _ _ _ _ _ _ (number of
statements answered) = _ _ _ _ _ _
Average score for this section

Transfer your score to the Hybrid
Solutions Index at the beginning of the
Self-Assessment.

CRITERION #2: DEFINE:

INTENT: Formulate the stakeholder problem. Define the problem, needs and objectives.

In my belief, the answer to this question is clearly defined:

5 Strongly Agree

4 Agree

3 Neutral

2 Disagree

1 Strongly Disagree

1. Who approved the Hybrid Solutions scope?
<--- Score

2. What was the context?
<--- Score

3. How did the Hybrid Solutions manager receive input to the development of a Hybrid Solutions improvement plan and the estimated completion

dates/times of each activity?
<--- Score

4. The political context: who holds power?
<--- Score

5. Will a Hybrid Solutions production readiness review
be required?
<--- Score

6. What critical content must be communicated –
who, what, when, where, and how?
<--- Score

7. Is there regularly 100% attendance at the team
meetings? If not, have appointed substitutes
attended to preserve cross-functionality and full
representation?
<--- Score

**8. What Hybrid Solutions requirements should be
gathered?**
<--- Score

9. What is out of scope?
<--- Score

10. Are approval levels defined for contracts and
supplements to contracts?
<--- Score

11. What are the record-keeping requirements of
Hybrid Solutions activities?
<--- Score

12. Are customer(s) identified and segmented

according to their different needs and requirements?
<--- Score

13. Is there a Hybrid Solutions management charter, including stakeholder case, problem and goal statements, scope, milestones, roles and responsibilities, communication plan?
<--- Score

14. What is the scope of the Hybrid Solutions work?
<--- Score

15. Are there any constraints known that bear on the ability to perform Hybrid Solutions work? How is the team addressing them?
<--- Score

16. Have all of the relationships been defined properly?
<--- Score

17. Where can you gather more information?
<--- Score

18. How do you gather Hybrid Solutions requirements?
<--- Score

19. Is there a critical path to deliver Hybrid Solutions results?
<--- Score

20. Is data collected and displayed to better understand customer(s) critical needs and requirements.
<--- Score

21. Is Hybrid Solutions currently on schedule according to the plan?
<--- Score

22. Is the work to date meeting requirements?
<--- Score

23. Is there any additional Hybrid Solutions definition of success?
<--- Score

24. What scope to assess?
<--- Score

25. How do you catch Hybrid Solutions definition inconsistencies?
<--- Score

26. What constraints exist that might impact the team?
<--- Score

27. What are (control) requirements for Hybrid Solutions Information?
<--- Score

28. Has the Hybrid Solutions work been fairly and/ or equitably divided and delegated among team members who are qualified and capable to perform the work? Has everyone contributed?
<--- Score

29. Do you have organizational privacy requirements?
<--- Score

30. Who is gathering information?
<--- Score

31. Will team members perform Hybrid Solutions work when assigned and in a timely fashion?
<--- Score

32. Are there different segments of customers?
<--- Score

33. Are different versions of process maps needed to account for the different types of inputs?
<--- Score

34. Has anyone else (internal or external to the group) attempted to solve this problem or a similar one before? If so, what knowledge can be leveraged from these previous efforts?
<--- Score

35. What system do you use for gathering Hybrid Solutions information?
<--- Score

36. How was the 'as is' process map developed, reviewed, verified and validated?
<--- Score

37. Is there a completed, verified, and validated high-level 'as is' (not 'should be' or 'could be') stakeholder process map?
<--- Score

38. Is there a completed SIPOC representation, describing the Suppliers, Inputs, Process, Outputs, and Customers?

<--- Score

39. Has the improvement team collected the 'voice of the customer' (obtained feedback – qualitative and quantitative)?
<--- Score

40. How is the team tracking and documenting its work?
<--- Score

41. How have you defined all Hybrid Solutions requirements first?
<--- Score

42. Will team members regularly document their Hybrid Solutions work?
<--- Score

43. What are the Hybrid Solutions use cases?
<--- Score

44. Are task requirements clearly defined?
<--- Score

45. Who are the Hybrid Solutions improvement team members, including Management Leads and Coaches?
<--- Score

46. Has the direction changed at all during the course of Hybrid Solutions? If so, when did it change and why?
<--- Score

47. Is Hybrid Solutions linked to key stakeholder goals

and objectives?
<--- Score

48. How do you gather the stories?
<--- Score

49. What is the scope?
<--- Score

50. How would you define Hybrid Solutions leadership?
<--- Score

51. How do you manage changes in Hybrid Solutions requirements?
<--- Score

52. What is the scope of Hybrid Solutions?
<--- Score

53. What are the Roles and Responsibilities for each team member and its leadership? Where is this documented?
<--- Score

54. Who is gathering Hybrid Solutions information?
<--- Score

55. Do you all define Hybrid Solutions in the same way?
<--- Score

56. How do you hand over Hybrid Solutions context?
<--- Score

57. What sources do you use to gather information for

a Hybrid Solutions study?

<--- Score

58. How does the Hybrid Solutions manager ensure against scope creep?

<--- Score

59. What key stakeholder process output measure(s) does Hybrid Solutions leverage and how?

<--- Score

60. How will the Hybrid Solutions team and the group measure complete success of Hybrid Solutions?

<--- Score

61. Has a Hybrid Solutions requirement not been met?

<--- Score

62. Do you have a Hybrid Solutions success story or case study ready to tell and share?

<--- Score

63. Are all requirements met?

<--- Score

64. Has a team charter been developed and communicated?

<--- Score

65. How will variation in the actual durations of each activity be dealt with to ensure that the expected Hybrid Solutions results are met?

<--- Score

66. Do the problem and goal statements meet the SMART criteria (specific, measurable, attainable,

relevant, and time-bound)?
<--- Score

67. How do you keep key subject matter experts in the loop?
<--- Score

68. How do you manage scope?
<--- Score

69. Has everyone on the team, including the team leaders, been properly trained?
<--- Score

70. What Hybrid Solutions services do you require?
<--- Score

71. Does the team have regular meetings?
<--- Score

72. Is scope creep really all bad news?
<--- Score

73. Are required metrics defined, what are they?
<--- Score

74. Are audit criteria, scope, frequency and methods defined?
<--- Score

75. Is the Hybrid Solutions scope manageable?
<--- Score

76. In what way can you redefine the criteria of choice clients have in your category in your favor?
<--- Score

77. How can the value of Hybrid Solutions be defined?
<--- Score

78. What are the rough order estimates on cost savings/opportunities that Hybrid Solutions brings?
<--- Score

79. Have the customer needs been translated into specific, measurable requirements? How?
<--- Score

80. Is Hybrid Solutions required?
<--- Score

81. What would be the goal or target for a Hybrid Solutions's improvement team?
<--- Score

82. What information do you gather?
<--- Score

83. What are the tasks and definitions?
<--- Score

84. Is the team adequately staffed with the desired cross-functionality? If not, what additional resources are available to the team?
<--- Score

85. How are consistent Hybrid Solutions definitions important?
<--- Score

86. When is/was the Hybrid Solutions start date?

<--- Score

87. What scope do you want your strategy to cover?
<--- Score

88. What is the worst case scenario?
<--- Score

89. How would you define the culture at your organization, how susceptible is it to Hybrid Solutions changes?
<--- Score

90. Have all basic functions of Hybrid Solutions been defined?
<--- Score

91. What sort of initial information to gather?
<--- Score

92. When are meeting minutes sent out? Who is on the distribution list?
<--- Score

93. Is the team equipped with available and reliable resources?
<--- Score

94. Are accountability and ownership for Hybrid Solutions clearly defined?
<--- Score

95. What specifically is the problem? Where does it occur? When does it occur? What is its extent?
<--- Score

96. Is full participation by members in regularly held team meetings guaranteed?
<--- Score

97. Is the improvement team aware of the different versions of a process: what they think it is vs. what it actually is vs. what it should be vs. what it could be?
<--- Score

98. What intelligence can you gather?
<--- Score

99. Does the scope remain the same?
<--- Score

100. What happens if Hybrid Solutions's scope changes?
<--- Score

101. Is special Hybrid Solutions user knowledge required?
<--- Score

102. What are the core elements of the Hybrid Solutions business case?
<--- Score

103. Has a high-level 'as is' process map been completed, verified and validated?
<--- Score

104. Why are you doing Hybrid Solutions and what is the scope?
<--- Score

105. What is in the scope and what is not in scope?

<--- Score

106. What information should you gather?
<--- Score

107. What are the Hybrid Solutions tasks and
definitions?
<--- Score

108. How do you build the right business case?
<--- Score

109. What is out-of-scope initially?
<--- Score

110. Is the scope of Hybrid Solutions defined?
<--- Score

111. What is the definition of Hybrid Solutions
excellence?
<--- Score

112. Is it clearly defined in and to your organization
what you do?
<--- Score

113. What is the context?
<--- Score

114. What are the dynamics of the communication
plan?
<--- Score

115. Has/have the customer(s) been identified?
<--- Score

116. Have specific policy objectives been defined?
<--- Score

117. Scope of sensitive information?
<--- Score

118. Are improvement team members fully trained on Hybrid Solutions?
<--- Score

119. Are roles and responsibilities formally defined?
<--- Score

120. What are the boundaries of the scope? What is in bounds and what is not? What is the start point? What is the stop point?
<--- Score

121. Has a project plan, Gantt chart, or similar been developed/completed?
<--- Score

122. If substitutes have been appointed, have they been briefed on the Hybrid Solutions goals and received regular communications as to the progress to date?
<--- Score

123. What customer feedback methods were used to solicit their input?
<--- Score

124. Are the Hybrid Solutions requirements complete?
<--- Score

125. What are the requirements for audit information?

<--- Score

126. Who defines (or who defined) the rules and roles?
<--- Score

127. How often are the team meetings?
<--- Score

128. What is a worst-case scenario for losses?
<--- Score

129. What defines best in class?
<--- Score

130. Is the Hybrid Solutions scope complete and appropriately sized?
<--- Score

131. Is there a clear Hybrid Solutions case definition?
<--- Score

132. What baselines are required to be defined and managed?
<--- Score

133. What are the compelling stakeholder reasons for embarking on Hybrid Solutions?
<--- Score

134. Are the Hybrid Solutions requirements testable?
<--- Score

135. How do you manage unclear Hybrid Solutions requirements?
<--- Score

136. Is the current 'as is' process being followed? If not, what are the discrepancies?
<--- Score

137. When is the estimated completion date?
<--- Score

138. Has your scope been defined?
<--- Score

Add up total points for this section:
_ _ _ _ _ = Total points for this section

Divided by: _ _ _ _ _ _ (number of statements answered) = _ _ _ _ _ _
Average score for this section

Transfer your score to the Hybrid Solutions Index at the beginning of the Self-Assessment.

CRITERION #3: MEASURE:

INTENT: Gather the correct data.
Measure the current performance and
evolution of the situation.

In my belief, the answer to this
question is clearly defined:

5 Strongly Agree

4 Agree

3 Neutral

2 Disagree

1 Strongly Disagree

1. How do you verify if Hybrid Solutions is built right?
<--- Score

2. Was a business case (cost/benefit) developed?
<--- Score

3. How do you verify performance?
<--- Score

4. What harm might be caused?
<--- Score

5. What are the estimated costs of proposed changes?
<--- Score

6. Will Hybrid Solutions have an impact on current business continuity, disaster recovery processes and/ or infrastructure?
<--- Score

7. Does management have the right priorities among projects?
<--- Score

8. What potential environmental factors impact the Hybrid Solutions effort?
<--- Score

9. What tests verify requirements?
<--- Score

10. What are the costs and benefits?
<--- Score

11. Are there competing Hybrid Solutions priorities?
<--- Score

12. What causes extra work or rework?
<--- Score

13. How do you aggregate measures across priorities?
<--- Score

14. Are missed Hybrid Solutions opportunities costing

your organization money?

<--- Score

15. Did you tackle the cause or the symptom?

<--- Score

16. How will costs be allocated?

<--- Score

17. What is the root cause(s) of the problem?

<--- Score

18. What are the operational costs after Hybrid Solutions deployment?

<--- Score

19. Is it possible to estimate the impact of unanticipated complexity such as wrong or failed assumptions, feedback, etcetera on proposed reforms?

<--- Score

20. How do you prevent mis-estimating cost?

<--- Score

21. What does your operating model cost?

<--- Score

22. Which measures and indicators matter?

<--- Score

23. What are the current costs of the Hybrid Solutions process?

<--- Score

24. Are actual costs in line with budgeted costs?

<--- Score

25. What are your customers expectations and measures?

<--- Score

26. What causes mismanagement?

<--- Score

27. What are you verifying?

<--- Score

28. How sensitive must the Hybrid Solutions strategy be to cost?

<--- Score

29. Are you aware of what could cause a problem?

<--- Score

30. Among the Hybrid Solutions product and service cost to be estimated, which is considered hardest to estimate?

<--- Score

31. How will measures be used to manage and adapt?

<--- Score

32. What users will be impacted?

<--- Score

33. How do you measure success?

<--- Score

34. What is the cost of rework?

<--- Score

35. How do you verify and develop ideas and innovations?
<--- Score

36. What is your Hybrid Solutions quality cost segregation study?
<--- Score

37. How are costs allocated?
<--- Score

38. What are the uncertainties surrounding estimates of impact?
<--- Score

39. How will you measure your Hybrid Solutions effectiveness?
<--- Score

40. How do you measure efficient delivery of Hybrid Solutions services?
<--- Score

41. Do you effectively measure and reward individual and team performance?
<--- Score

42. Who should receive measurement reports?
<--- Score

43. How can a Hybrid Solutions test verify your ideas or assumptions?
<--- Score

44. Are indirect costs charged to the Hybrid

Solutions program?
<--- Score

45. Has a cost center been established?
<--- Score

46. What details are required of the Hybrid Solutions cost structure?
<--- Score

47. How much does it cost?
<--- Score

48. What is the Hybrid Solutions business impact?
<--- Score

49. Does the Hybrid Solutions task fit the client's priorities?
<--- Score

50. What do people want to verify?
<--- Score

51. Do you have any cost Hybrid Solutions limitation requirements?
<--- Score

52. Are you able to realize any cost savings?
<--- Score

53. Do you verify that corrective actions were taken?
<--- Score

54. Are there any easy-to-implement alternatives to Hybrid Solutions? Sometimes other solutions are available that do not require the cost implications of a

full-blown project?

<--- Score

55. What are allowable costs?

<--- Score

56. What disadvantage does this cause for the user?

<--- Score

57. What is your decision requirements diagram?

<--- Score

58. How will your organization measure success?

<--- Score

59. How can you reduce the costs of obtaining inputs?

<--- Score

60. How is the value delivered by Hybrid Solutions being measured?

<--- Score

61. Is the cost worth the Hybrid Solutions effort ?

<--- Score

62. Why do you expend time and effort to implement measurement, for whom?

<--- Score

63. How can you measure Hybrid Solutions in a systematic way?

<--- Score

64. What are the costs of reform?

<--- Score

65. What does losing customers cost your organization?
<--- Score

66. What are your key Hybrid Solutions organizational performance measures, including key short and longer-term financial measures?
<--- Score

67. Have design-to-cost goals been established?
<--- Score

68. Do you have an issue in getting priority?
<--- Score

69. What is the total cost related to deploying Hybrid Solutions, including any consulting or professional services?
<--- Score

70. How is progress measured?
<--- Score

71. What could cause delays in the schedule?
<--- Score

72. What is measured? Why?
<--- Score

73. Is the solution cost-effective?
<--- Score

74. Where is it measured?
<--- Score

75. What would it cost to replace your technology?
<--- Score

76. Which Hybrid Solutions impacts are significant?
<--- Score

77. What do you measure and why?
<--- Score

78. What evidence is there and what is measured?
<--- Score

79. Are there measurements based on task performance?
<--- Score

80. Is there an opportunity to verify requirements?
<--- Score

81. Do you have a flow diagram of what happens?
<--- Score

82. How do your measurements capture actionable Hybrid Solutions information for use in exceeding your customers expectations and securing your customers engagement?
<--- Score

83. What is an unallowable cost?
<--- Score

84. What are the strategic priorities for this year?
<--- Score

85. Who pays the cost?

<--- Score

86. When should you bother with diagrams?
<--- Score

87. What are the costs of delaying Hybrid Solutions action?
<--- Score

88. What are the Hybrid Solutions key cost drivers?
<--- Score

89. What does a Test Case verify?
<--- Score

90. Are the Hybrid Solutions benefits worth its costs?
<--- Score

91. How do you verify the authenticity of the data and information used?
<--- Score

92. Do you aggressively reward and promote the people who have the biggest impact on creating excellent Hybrid Solutions services/products?
<--- Score

93. How do you quantify and qualify impacts?
<--- Score

94. Do the benefits outweigh the costs?
<--- Score

95. What is the total fixed cost?
<--- Score

96. Are the measurements objective?

<--- Score

97. What are your operating costs?

<--- Score

98. What happens if cost savings do not materialize?

<--- Score

99. When are costs are incurred?

<--- Score

100. How can you manage cost down?

<--- Score

101. How do you control the overall costs of your work processes?

<--- Score

102. Which costs should be taken into account?

<--- Score

103. How do you verify and validate the Hybrid Solutions data?

<--- Score

104. Why do the measurements/indicators matter?

<--- Score

105. What measurements are being captured?

<--- Score

106. What are the Hybrid Solutions investment costs?

<--- Score

107. What are the types and number of measures

to use?
<--- Score

108. How are measurements made?
<--- Score

109. How can you reduce costs?
<--- Score

110. What are your primary costs, revenues, assets?
<--- Score

111. What methods are feasible and acceptable to estimate the impact of reforms?
<--- Score

112. Are supply costs steady or fluctuating?
<--- Score

113. How do you verify the Hybrid Solutions requirements quality?
<--- Score

114. What relevant entities could be measured?
<--- Score

115. How will success or failure be measured?
<--- Score

116. Have you included everything in your Hybrid Solutions cost models?
<--- Score

117. Are the units of measure consistent?
<--- Score

118. How will effects be measured?
<--- Score

119. What drives O&M cost?
<--- Score

120. What is the cause of any Hybrid Solutions gaps?
<--- Score

121. What causes investor action?
<--- Score

122. What could cause you to change course?
<--- Score

123. Have you made assumptions about the shape of the future, particularly its impact on your customers and competitors?
<--- Score

124. Where is the cost?
<--- Score

125. What are the costs?
<--- Score

126. When a disaster occurs, who gets priority?
<--- Score

127. Who is involved in verifying compliance?
<--- Score

128. How do you measure lifecycle phases?
<--- Score

129. How do you measure variability?
<--- Score

130. Are Hybrid Solutions vulnerabilities categorized and prioritized?
<--- Score

131. How frequently do you track Hybrid Solutions measures?
<--- Score

132. What can be used to verify compliance?
<--- Score

133. At what cost?
<--- Score

Add up total points for this section:
_ _ _ _ _ = Total points for this section

Divided by: _ _ _ _ _ _ (number of statements answered) = _ _ _ _ _ _ Average score for this section

Transfer your score to the Hybrid Solutions Index at the beginning of the Self-Assessment.

CRITERION #4: ANALYZE:

INTENT: Analyze causes, assumptions and hypotheses.

In my belief, the answer to this question is clearly defined:

5 Strongly Agree

4 Agree

3 Neutral

2 Disagree

1 Strongly Disagree

1. Who will gather what data?
<--- Score

2. Are Hybrid Solutions changes recognized early enough to be approved through the regular process?
<--- Score

3. What is your organizations system for selecting qualified vendors?

<--- Score

4. What were the crucial 'moments of truth' on the process map?
<--- Score

5. Where is Hybrid Solutions data gathered?
<--- Score

6. What Hybrid Solutions data should be collected?
<--- Score

7. How has the Hybrid Solutions data been gathered?
<--- Score

8. Do your contracts/agreements contain data security obligations?
<--- Score

9. What successful thing are you doing today that may be blinding you to new growth opportunities?
<--- Score

10. Do several people in different organizational units assist with the Hybrid Solutions process?
<--- Score

11. What is your organizations process which leads to recognition of value generation?
<--- Score

12. How are outputs preserved and protected?
<--- Score

13. Did any additional data need to be collected?

<--- Score

14. Were there any improvement opportunities identified from the process analysis?
<--- Score

15. What other jobs or tasks affect the performance of the steps in the Hybrid Solutions process?
<--- Score

16. What is the complexity of the output produced?
<--- Score

17. What Hybrid Solutions data will be collected?
<--- Score

18. What Hybrid Solutions data should be managed?
<--- Score

19. What output to create?
<--- Score

20. Think about the functions involved in your Hybrid Solutions project, what processes flow from these functions?
<--- Score

21. Is the Hybrid Solutions process severely broken such that a re-design is necessary?
<--- Score

22. What qualifications are needed?
<--- Score

23. What were the financial benefits resulting from any 'ground fruit or low-hanging fruit' (quick fixes)?

<--- Score

24. How is the way you as the leader think and process information affecting your organizational culture?
<--- Score

25. Can you add value to the current Hybrid Solutions decision-making process (largely qualitative) by incorporating uncertainty modeling (more quantitative)?
<--- Score

26. How will the data be checked for quality?
<--- Score

27. What systems/processes must you excel at?
<--- Score

28. What are the processes for audit reporting and management?
<--- Score

29. What resources go in to get the desired output?
<--- Score

30. How do your work systems and key work processes relate to and capitalize on your core competencies?
<--- Score

31. Is there a strict change management process?
<--- Score

32. How will the Hybrid Solutions data be captured?
<--- Score

33. What qualifications are necessary?
<--- Score

34. What kind of crime could a potential new hire have committed that would not only not disqualify him/her from being hired by your organization, but would actually indicate that he/she might be a particularly good fit?
<--- Score

35. Have the problem and goal statements been updated to reflect the additional knowledge gained from the analyze phase?
<--- Score

36. Who is involved in the management review process?
<--- Score

37. What is the output?
<--- Score

38. An organizationally feasible system request is one that considers the mission, goals and objectives of the organization, key questions are: is the Hybrid Solutions solution request practical and will it solve a problem or take advantage of an opportunity to achieve company goals?
<--- Score

39. How do you implement and manage your work processes to ensure that they meet design requirements?
<--- Score

40. What are the Hybrid Solutions business drivers?

<--- Score

41. What qualifications and skills do you need?

<--- Score

42. What, related to, Hybrid Solutions processes does your organization outsource?

<--- Score

43. Think about some of the processes you undertake within your organization, which do you own?

<--- Score

44. What are your best practices for minimizing Hybrid Solutions project risk, while demonstrating incremental value and quick wins throughout the Hybrid Solutions project lifecycle?

<--- Score

45. How do you measure the operational performance of your key work systems and processes, including productivity, cycle time, and other appropriate measures of process effectiveness, efficiency, and innovation?

<--- Score

46. What training and qualifications will you need?

<--- Score

47. How is Hybrid Solutions data gathered?

<--- Score

48. Do your employees have the opportunity to do what they do best everyday?

<--- Score

49. What tools were used to narrow the list of possible causes?
<--- Score

50. What are your current levels and trends in key Hybrid Solutions measures or indicators of product and process performance that are important to and directly serve your customers?
<--- Score

51. Was a cause-and-effect diagram used to explore the different types of causes (or sources of variation)?
<--- Score

52. What tools were used to generate the list of possible causes?
<--- Score

53. What process improvements will be needed?
<--- Score

54. Are all team members qualified for all tasks?
<--- Score

55. Were Pareto charts (or similar) used to portray the 'heavy hitters' (or key sources of variation)?
<--- Score

56. Should you invest in industry-recognized qualifications?
<--- Score

57. What quality tools were used to get through the analyze phase?

<--- Score

58. Who qualifies to gain access to data?
<--- Score

59. How often will data be collected for measures?
<--- Score

60. A compounding model resolution with available relevant data can often provide insight towards a solution methodology; which Hybrid Solutions models, tools and techniques are necessary?
<--- Score

61. Do quality systems drive continuous improvement?
<--- Score

62. How do you use Hybrid Solutions data and information to support organizational decision making and innovation?
<--- Score

63. Are your outputs consistent?
<--- Score

64. What is the oversight process?
<--- Score

65. What controls do you have in place to protect data?
<--- Score

66. What are the best opportunities for value improvement?
<--- Score

67. Who is involved with workflow mapping?
<--- Score

68. Is the performance gap determined?
<--- Score

69. What are your Hybrid Solutions processes?
<--- Score

70. Have you defined which data is gathered how?
<--- Score

71. Do you have the authority to produce the output?
<--- Score

72. What methods do you use to gather Hybrid Solutions data?
<--- Score

73. How does the organization define, manage, and improve its Hybrid Solutions processes?
<--- Score

74. How difficult is it to qualify what Hybrid Solutions ROI is?
<--- Score

75. Identify an operational issue in your organization, for example, could a particular task be done more quickly or more efficiently by Hybrid Solutions?
<--- Score

76. What types of data do your Hybrid Solutions indicators require?

<--- Score

77. How is the data gathered?
<--- Score

78. What internal processes need improvement?
<--- Score

79. How is the Hybrid Solutions Value Stream Mapping managed?
<--- Score

80. What will drive Hybrid Solutions change?
<--- Score

81. Was a detailed process map created to amplify critical steps of the 'as is' stakeholder process?
<--- Score

82. What are the revised rough estimates of the financial savings/opportunity for Hybrid Solutions improvements?
<--- Score

83. What are your outputs?
<--- Score

84. What Hybrid Solutions metrics are outputs of the process?
<--- Score

85. Were any designed experiments used to generate additional insight into the data analysis?
<--- Score

86. Do you understand your management processes

today?
<--- Score

87. What are the disruptive Hybrid Solutions technologies that enable your organization to radically change your business processes?
<--- Score

88. Is the gap/opportunity displayed and communicated in financial terms?
<--- Score

89. Record-keeping requirements flow from the records needed as inputs, outputs, controls and for transformation of a Hybrid Solutions process, are the records needed as inputs to the Hybrid Solutions process available?
<--- Score

90. What Hybrid Solutions data do you gather or use now?
<--- Score

91. Is there an established change management process?
<--- Score

92. Is there any way to speed up the process?
<--- Score

93. How much data can be collected in the given timeframe?
<--- Score

94. Are all staff in core Hybrid Solutions subjects Highly Qualified?

<--- Score

95. Did any value-added analysis or 'lean thinking' take place to identify some of the gaps shown on the 'as is' process map?
<--- Score

96. What does the data say about the performance of the stakeholder process?
<--- Score

97. When should a process be art not science?
<--- Score

98. Is pre-qualification of suppliers carried out?
<--- Score

99. What information qualified as important?
<--- Score

100. Do you, as a leader, bounce back quickly from setbacks?
<--- Score

101. Which Hybrid Solutions data should be retained?
<--- Score

102. What qualifications do Hybrid Solutions leaders need?
<--- Score

103. What qualifies as competition?
<--- Score

104. Have any additional benefits been identified that

will result from closing all or most of the gaps?
<--- Score

105. How do you define collaboration and team output?
<--- Score

106. What did the team gain from developing a sub-process map?
<--- Score

107. Is the final output clearly identified?
<--- Score

108. How was the detailed process map generated, verified, and validated?
<--- Score

109. Do staff qualifications match your project?
<--- Score

110. Has an output goal been set?
<--- Score

111. What is the cost of poor quality as supported by the team's analysis?
<--- Score

112. What process should you select for improvement?
<--- Score

113. Where can you get qualified talent today?
<--- Score

114. How do mission and objectives affect the Hybrid

Solutions processes of your organization?
<--- Score

115. Do your leaders quickly bounce back from setbacks?
<--- Score

116. How will corresponding data be collected?
<--- Score

117. How will the change process be managed?
<--- Score

118. Is the required Hybrid Solutions data gathered?
<--- Score

119. What data do you need to collect?
<--- Score

120. How do you ensure that the Hybrid Solutions opportunity is realistic?
<--- Score

121. Is data and process analysis, root cause analysis and quantifying the gap/opportunity in place?
<--- Score

122. Is the suppliers process defined and controlled?
<--- Score

123. What are the Hybrid Solutions design outputs?
<--- Score

124. What is the Hybrid Solutions Driver?
<--- Score

125. Who gets your output?
<--- Score

126. What other organizational variables, such as reward systems or communication systems, affect the performance of this Hybrid Solutions process?
<--- Score

127. What do you need to qualify?
<--- Score

128. Are you missing Hybrid Solutions opportunities?
<--- Score

129. What are the necessary qualifications?
<--- Score

130. What are evaluation criteria for the output?
<--- Score

131. What conclusions were drawn from the team's data collection and analysis? How did the team reach these conclusions?
<--- Score

132. What data is gathered?
<--- Score

133. How do you identify specific Hybrid Solutions investment opportunities and emerging trends?
<--- Score

134. Has data output been validated?
<--- Score

135. Where is the data coming from to measure compliance?

<--- Score

136. How many input/output points does it require?

<--- Score

137. What are your current levels and trends in key measures or indicators of Hybrid Solutions product and process performance that are important to and directly serve your customers? How do these results compare with the performance of your competitors and other organizations with similar offerings?

<--- Score

138. What are the personnel training and qualifications required?

<--- Score

139. How can risk management be tied procedurally to process elements?

<--- Score

Add up total points for this section:

_ _ _ _ _ = Total points for this section

Divided by: _ _ _ _ _ _ (number of statements answered) = _ _ _ _ _ _ Average score for this section

Transfer your score to the Hybrid Solutions Index at the beginning of the Self-Assessment.

CRITERION #5: IMPROVE:

INTENT: Develop a practical solution. Innovate, establish and test the solution and to measure the results.

In my belief, the answer to this question is clearly defined:

5 Strongly Agree

4 Agree

3 Neutral

2 Disagree

1 Strongly Disagree

1. What Hybrid Solutions improvements can be made?
<--- Score

2. Who are the Hybrid Solutions decision-makers?
<--- Score

3. Are the risks fully understood, reasonable and manageable?
<--- Score

4. Is the scope clearly documented?
<--- Score

5. What is the team's contingency plan for potential problems occurring in implementation?
<--- Score

6. How do you go about comparing Hybrid Solutions approaches/solutions?
<--- Score

7. Is the measure of success for Hybrid Solutions understandable to a variety of people?
<--- Score

8. What is the magnitude of the improvements?
<--- Score

9. What is the Hybrid Solutions's sustainability risk?
<--- Score

10. Who will be responsible for making the decisions to include or exclude requested changes once Hybrid Solutions is underway?
<--- Score

11. What were the underlying assumptions on the cost-benefit analysis?
<--- Score

12. Would you develop a Hybrid Solutions Communication Strategy?
<--- Score

13. What tools were used to evaluate the potential

solutions?

<--- Score

14. In the past few months, what is the smallest change you have made that has had the biggest positive result? What was it about that small change that produced the large return?

<--- Score

15. How can skill-level changes improve Hybrid Solutions?

<--- Score

16. Who controls the risk?

<--- Score

17. Do you need to do a usability evaluation?

<--- Score

18. Are decisions made in a timely manner?

<--- Score

19. To what extent does management recognize Hybrid Solutions as a tool to increase the results?

<--- Score

20. Is the Hybrid Solutions documentation thorough?

<--- Score

21. What can you do to improve?

<--- Score

22. Which of the recognised risks out of all risks can be most likely transferred?

<--- Score

23. What were the criteria for evaluating a Hybrid Solutions pilot?
<--- Score

24. Are risk management tasks balanced centrally and locally?
<--- Score

25. What are the concrete Hybrid Solutions results?
<--- Score

26. What is the risk?
<--- Score

27. How do you manage and improve your Hybrid Solutions work systems to deliver customer value and achieve organizational success and sustainability?
<--- Score

28. How do you link measurement and risk?
<--- Score

29. Does the goal represent a desired result that can be measured?
<--- Score

30. Does a good decision guarantee a good outcome?
<--- Score

31. What is the implementation plan?
<--- Score

32. Is supporting Hybrid Solutions documentation

required?
<--- Score

33. What resources are required for the improvement efforts?
<--- Score

34. What error proofing will be done to address some of the discrepancies observed in the 'as is' process?
<--- Score

35. What to do with the results or outcomes of measurements?
<--- Score

36. How are Hybrid Solutions risks managed?
<--- Score

37. What should a proof of concept or pilot accomplish?
<--- Score

38. Is any Hybrid Solutions documentation required?
<--- Score

39. Where do you need Hybrid Solutions improvement?
<--- Score

40. What improvements have been achieved?
<--- Score

41. Who do you report Hybrid Solutions results to?
<--- Score

42. What area needs the greatest improvement?

<--- Score

43. Do you combine technical expertise with business knowledge and Hybrid Solutions Key topics include lifecycles, development approaches, requirements and how to make a business case?
<--- Score

44. Why improve in the first place?
<--- Score

45. If you could go back in time five years, what decision would you make differently? What is your best guess as to what decision you're making today you might regret five years from now?
<--- Score

46. Is the solution technically practical?
<--- Score

47. How will you know that a change is an improvement?
<--- Score

48. Do you cover the five essential competencies: Communication, Collaboration,Innovation, Adaptability, and Leadership that improve an organizations ability to leverage the new Hybrid Solutions in a volatile global economy?
<--- Score

49. Who should make the Hybrid Solutions decisions?
<--- Score

50. What communications are necessary to support the implementation of the solution?

<--- Score

51. Will the controls trigger any other risks?
<--- Score

52. For decision problems, how do you develop a decision statement?
<--- Score

53. How scalable is your Hybrid Solutions solution?
<--- Score

54. How do you mitigate Hybrid Solutions risk?
<--- Score

55. What do you want to improve?
<--- Score

56. Risk factors: what are the characteristics of Hybrid Solutions that make it risky?
<--- Score

57. What are the affordable Hybrid Solutions risks?
<--- Score

58. What current systems have to be understood and/ or changed?
<--- Score

59. What are your current levels and trends in key measures or indicators of workforce and leader development?
<--- Score

60. How do the Hybrid Solutions results compare

with the performance of your competitors and other organizations with similar offerings?
<--- Score

61. How do you measure risk?
<--- Score

62. Hybrid Solutions risk decisions: whose call Is It?
<--- Score

63. Do you have the optimal project management team structure?
<--- Score

64. What criteria will you use to assess your Hybrid Solutions risks?
<--- Score

65. What is Hybrid Solutions risk?
<--- Score

66. What practices helps your organization to develop its capacity to recognize patterns?
<--- Score

67. What actually has to improve and by how much?
<--- Score

68. What needs improvement? Why?
<--- Score

69. What assumptions are made about the solution and approach?
<--- Score

70. Is Hybrid Solutions documentation maintained?

<--- Score

71. How is continuous improvement applied to risk management?
<--- Score

72. What tools were used to tap into the creativity and encourage 'outside the box' thinking?
<--- Score

73. How do you improve Hybrid Solutions service perception, and satisfaction?
<--- Score

74. Is there any other Hybrid Solutions solution?
<--- Score

75. What tools were most useful during the improve phase?
<--- Score

76. Who will be responsible for documenting the Hybrid Solutions requirements in detail?
<--- Score

77. How do you improve your likelihood of success ?
<--- Score

78. What lessons, if any, from a pilot were incorporated into the design of the full-scale solution?
<--- Score

79. Are you assessing Hybrid Solutions and risk?
<--- Score

80. How do you improve productivity?

<--- Score

81. Is risk periodically assessed?
<--- Score

82. What is Hybrid Solutions's impact on utilizing the best solution(s)?
<--- Score

83. Who are the people involved in developing and implementing Hybrid Solutions?
<--- Score

84. How do you decide how much to remunerate an employee?
<--- Score

85. Can the solution be designed and implemented within an acceptable time period?
<--- Score

86. Are procedures documented for managing Hybrid Solutions risks?
<--- Score

87. How can you improve Hybrid Solutions?
<--- Score

88. What are the implications of the one critical Hybrid Solutions decision 10 minutes, 10 months, and 10 years from now?
<--- Score

89. Are risk triggers captured?
<--- Score

90. What risks do you need to manage?
<--- Score

91. Are the most efficient solutions problem-specific?
<--- Score

92. Can you identify any significant risks or exposures to Hybrid Solutions third- parties (vendors, service providers, alliance partners etc) that concern you?
<--- Score

93. For estimation problems, how do you develop an estimation statement?
<--- Score

94. Is the Hybrid Solutions solution sustainable?
<--- Score

95. How do you measure progress and evaluate training effectiveness?
<--- Score

96. How do you deal with Hybrid Solutions risk?
<--- Score

97. Do vendor agreements bring new compliance risk ?
<--- Score

98. How can the phases of Hybrid Solutions development be identified?
<--- Score

99. How can you improve performance?
<--- Score

100. What are the Hybrid Solutions security risks?
<--- Score

101. Is there a high likelihood that any recommendations will achieve their intended results?
<--- Score

102. Where do the Hybrid Solutions decisions reside?
<--- Score

103. How will you recognize and celebrate results?
<--- Score

104. Risk events: what are the things that could go wrong?
<--- Score

105. Who will be using the results of the measurement activities?
<--- Score

106. How do you define the solutions' scope?
<--- Score

107. How is knowledge sharing about risk management improved?
<--- Score

108. Who manages Hybrid Solutions risk?
<--- Score

109. When you map the key players in your own work and the types/domains of relationships with them, which relationships do you find easy and which challenging, and why?

<--- Score

110. Do those selected for the Hybrid Solutions team have a good general understanding of what Hybrid Solutions is all about?
<--- Score

111. How will you know that you have improved?
<--- Score

112. How are policy decisions made and where?
<--- Score

113. Who are the Hybrid Solutions decision makers?
<--- Score

114. How can you better manage risk?
<--- Score

115. What tools do you use once you have decided on a Hybrid Solutions strategy and more importantly how do you choose?
<--- Score

116. Which Hybrid Solutions solution is appropriate?
<--- Score

117. What does the 'should be' process map/design look like?
<--- Score

118. How will you measure the results?
<--- Score

119. Are events managed to resolution?
<--- Score

120. Have you achieved Hybrid Solutions improvements?
<--- Score

121. How do you keep improving Hybrid Solutions?
<--- Score

122. What are the expected Hybrid Solutions results?
<--- Score

123. Who makes the Hybrid Solutions decisions in your organization?
<--- Score

124. How do you measure improved Hybrid Solutions service perception, and satisfaction?
<--- Score

125. Was a Hybrid Solutions charter developed?
<--- Score

126. What alternative responses are available to manage risk?
<--- Score

127. At what point will vulnerability assessments be performed once Hybrid Solutions is put into production (e.g., ongoing Risk Management after implementation)?
<--- Score

128. Who controls key decisions that will be made?
<--- Score

129. How risky is your organization?

<--- Score

130. Risk Identification: What are the possible risk events your organization faces in relation to Hybrid Solutions?

<--- Score

131. How does your organization evaluate strategic Hybrid Solutions success?

<--- Score

132. How will you know when its improved?

<--- Score

Add up total points for this section:
_ _ _ _ _ = Total points for this section

Divided by: _ _ _ _ _ _ (number of statements answered) = _ _ _ _ _ _
Average score for this section

Transfer your score to the Hybrid Solutions Index at the beginning of the Self-Assessment.

CRITERION #6: CONTROL:

INTENT: Implement the practical solution. Maintain the performance and correct possible complications.

In my belief, the answer to this question is clearly defined:

5 Strongly Agree

4 Agree

3 Neutral

2 Disagree

1 Strongly Disagree

1. What is the recommended frequency of auditing?
<--- Score

2. How do you encourage people to take control and responsibility?
<--- Score

3. How do you establish and deploy modified action plans if circumstances require a shift in

plans and rapid execution of new plans?
<--- Score

4. Has the Hybrid Solutions value of standards been quantified?
<--- Score

5. Are there documented procedures?
<--- Score

6. How do you select, collect, align, and integrate Hybrid Solutions data and information for tracking daily operations and overall organizational performance, including progress relative to strategic objectives and action plans?
<--- Score

7. How will the process owner and team be able to hold the gains?
<--- Score

8. What should the next improvement project be that is related to Hybrid Solutions?
<--- Score

9. How will new or emerging customer needs/ requirements be checked/communicated to orient the process toward meeting the new specifications and continually reducing variation?
<--- Score

10. What are customers monitoring?
<--- Score

11. What other systems, operations, processes, and infrastructures (hiring practices, staffing, training,

incentives/rewards, metrics/dashboards/scorecards, etc.) need updates, additions, changes, or deletions in order to facilitate knowledge transfer and improvements?
<--- Score

12. How do senior leaders actions reflect a commitment to the organizations Hybrid Solutions values?
<--- Score

13. What are your results for key measures or indicators of the accomplishment of your Hybrid Solutions strategy and action plans, including building and strengthening core competencies?
<--- Score

14. How widespread is its use?
<--- Score

15. Who controls critical resources?
<--- Score

16. How do your controls stack up?
<--- Score

17. Have new or revised work instructions resulted?
<--- Score

18. How will you measure your QA plan's effectiveness?
<--- Score

19. How can you best use all of your knowledge repositories to enhance learning and sharing?
<--- Score

20. Are new process steps, standards, and documentation ingrained into normal operations?
<--- Score

21. How will Hybrid Solutions decisions be made and monitored?
<--- Score

22. Are the planned controls in place?
<--- Score

23. How will the day-to-day responsibilities for monitoring and continual improvement be transferred from the improvement team to the process owner?
<--- Score

24. Are the planned controls working?
<--- Score

25. How might the group capture best practices and lessons learned so as to leverage improvements?
<--- Score

26. Is there a transfer of ownership and knowledge to process owner and process team tasked with the responsibilities.
<--- Score

27. Is there documentation that will support the successful operation of the improvement?
<--- Score

28. How will report readings be checked to effectively monitor performance?

<--- Score

29. Implementation Planning: is a pilot needed to test the changes before a full roll out occurs?
<--- Score

30. Are documented procedures clear and easy to follow for the operators?
<--- Score

31. What should you measure to verify efficiency gains?
<--- Score

32. Does the Hybrid Solutions performance meet the customer's requirements?
<--- Score

33. What do you measure to verify effectiveness gains?
<--- Score

34. What is the control/monitoring plan?
<--- Score

35. How is change control managed?
<--- Score

36. What is your theory of human motivation, and how does your compensation plan fit with that view?
<--- Score

37. Does Hybrid Solutions appropriately measure and monitor risk?
<--- Score

38. Does the response plan contain a definite closed loop continual improvement scheme (e.g., plan-do-check-act)?
<--- Score

39. What can you control?
<--- Score

40. Will existing staff require re-training, for example, to learn new business processes?
<--- Score

41. Act/Adjust: What Do you Need to Do Differently?
<--- Score

42. How do you spread information?
<--- Score

43. Is knowledge gained on process shared and institutionalized?
<--- Score

44. Is reporting being used or needed?
<--- Score

45. Is there a documented and implemented monitoring plan?
<--- Score

46. Who sets the Hybrid Solutions standards?
<--- Score

47. What do your reports reflect?
<--- Score

48. Are the Hybrid Solutions standards challenging?

<--- Score

49. What are the key elements of your Hybrid Solutions performance improvement system, including your evaluation, organizational learning, and innovation processes?
<--- Score

50. Do the Hybrid Solutions decisions you make today help people and the planet tomorrow?
<--- Score

51. Is new knowledge gained imbedded in the response plan?
<--- Score

52. What are the known security controls?
<--- Score

53. What quality tools were useful in the control phase?
<--- Score

54. Will your goals reflect your program budget?
<--- Score

55. How do you plan for the cost of succession?
<--- Score

56. Who is the Hybrid Solutions process owner?
<--- Score

57. Do you monitor the effectiveness of your Hybrid Solutions activities?
<--- Score

58. Is there a Hybrid Solutions Communication plan covering who needs to get what information when?

<--- Score

59. How will input, process, and output variables be checked to detect for sub-optimal conditions?

<--- Score

60. What other areas of the group might benefit from the Hybrid Solutions team's improvements, knowledge, and learning?

<--- Score

61. Is there a standardized process?

<--- Score

62. What is the best design framework for Hybrid Solutions organization now that, in a post industrial-age if the top-down, command and control model is no longer relevant?

<--- Score

63. You may have created your quality measures at a time when you lacked resources, technology wasn't up to the required standard, or low service levels were the industry norm. Have those circumstances changed?

<--- Score

64. Will the team be available to assist members in planning investigations?

<--- Score

65. What do you stand for--and what are you against?

<--- Score

66. Can you adapt and adjust to changing Hybrid Solutions situations?
<--- Score

67. How likely is the current Hybrid Solutions plan to come in on schedule or on budget?
<--- Score

68. Is a response plan established and deployed?
<--- Score

69. Is there a recommended audit plan for routine surveillance inspections of Hybrid Solutions's gains?
<--- Score

70. Will any special training be provided for results interpretation?
<--- Score

71. What is your plan to assess your security risks?
<--- Score

72. Are suggested corrective/restorative actions indicated on the response plan for known causes to problems that might surface?
<--- Score

73. Is a response plan in place for when the input, process, or output measures indicate an 'out-of-control' condition?
<--- Score

74. How do you plan on providing proper recognition and disclosure of supporting companies?

<--- Score

75. How do controls support value?
<--- Score

76. Are controls in place and consistently applied?
<--- Score

77. Are pertinent alerts monitored, analyzed and distributed to appropriate personnel?
<--- Score

78. Can support from partners be adjusted?
<--- Score

79. Does a troubleshooting guide exist or is it needed?
<--- Score

80. In the case of a Hybrid Solutions project, the criteria for the audit derive from implementation objectives, an audit of a Hybrid Solutions project involves assessing whether the recommendations outlined for implementation have been met, can you track that any Hybrid Solutions project is implemented as planned, and is it working?
<--- Score

81. Does job training on the documented procedures need to be part of the process team's education and training?
<--- Score

82. Are operating procedures consistent?
<--- Score

83. Is there a control plan in place for sustaining

improvements (short and long-term)?
<--- Score

84. Has the improved process and its steps been standardized?
<--- Score

85. How will the process owner verify improvement in present and future sigma levels, process capabilities?
<--- Score

86. Is the Hybrid Solutions test/monitoring cost justified?
<--- Score

87. Are you measuring, monitoring and predicting Hybrid Solutions activities to optimize operations and profitability, and enhancing outcomes?
<--- Score

88. Who has control over resources?
<--- Score

89. Who is going to spread your message?
<--- Score

90. Is there an action plan in case of emergencies?
<--- Score

91. What are you attempting to measure/monitor?
<--- Score

92. What key inputs and outputs are being measured on an ongoing basis?
<--- Score

93. What Hybrid Solutions standards are applicable?
<--- Score

94. What are the critical parameters to watch?
<--- Score

Add up total points for this section:
_ _ _ _ _ = Total points for this section

Divided by: _ _ _ _ _ _ (number of
statements answered) = _ _ _ _ _ _
Average score for this section

Transfer your score to the Hybrid
Solutions Index at the beginning of the
Self-Assessment.

CRITERION #7: SUSTAIN:

INTENT: Retain the benefits.

In my belief, the answer to this question is clearly defined:

5 Strongly Agree

4 Agree

3 Neutral

2 Disagree

1 Strongly Disagree

1. Is your strategy driving your strategy? Or is the way in which you allocate resources driving your strategy?
<--- Score

2. What are the business goals Hybrid Solutions is aiming to achieve?
<--- Score

3. What are the rules and assumptions your industry operates under? What if the opposite

were true?

<--- Score

4. What is your competitive advantage?

<--- Score

5. What is the big Hybrid Solutions idea?

<--- Score

6. In retrospect, of the projects that you pulled the plug on, what percent do you wish had been allowed to keep going, and what percent do you wish had ended earlier?

<--- Score

7. What new services of functionality will be implemented next with Hybrid Solutions ?

<--- Score

8. How will you ensure you get what you expected?

<--- Score

9. What is the craziest thing you can do?

<--- Score

10. What is the funding source for this project?

<--- Score

11. What is a feasible sequencing of reform initiatives over time?

<--- Score

12. If your customer were your grandmother, would you tell her to buy what you're selling?

<--- Score

13. Who is the main stakeholder, with ultimate responsibility for driving Hybrid Solutions forward?
<--- Score

14. What are internal and external Hybrid Solutions relations?
<--- Score

15. What should you stop doing?
<--- Score

16. What must you excel at?
<--- Score

17. Which functions and people interact with the supplier and or customer?
<--- Score

18. Political -is anyone trying to undermine this project?
<--- Score

19. Which models, tools and techniques are necessary?
<--- Score

20. How do you track customer value, profitability or financial return, organizational success, and sustainability?
<--- Score

21. What potential megatrends could make your business model obsolete?
<--- Score

22. What trophy do you want on your mantle?

<--- Score

23. What is your Hybrid Solutions strategy?
<--- Score

24. What are the challenges?
<--- Score

25. How do you cross-sell and up-sell your Hybrid Solutions success?
<--- Score

26. Who do you want your customers to become?
<--- Score

27. What is your question? Why?
<--- Score

28. How do you manage Hybrid Solutions Knowledge Management (KM)?
<--- Score

29. Are new benefits received and understood?
<--- Score

30. What are the barriers to increased Hybrid Solutions production?
<--- Score

31. If you weren't already in this business, would you enter it today? And if not, what are you going to do about it?
<--- Score

32. What trouble can you get into?
<--- Score

33. Did your employees make progress today?
<--- Score

34. Is your basic point _____ or _____?
<--- Score

35. Ask yourself: how would you do this work if you only had one staff member to do it?
<--- Score

36. Are the criteria for selecting recommendations stated?
<--- Score

37. What are the short and long-term Hybrid Solutions goals?
<--- Score

38. What may be the consequences for the performance of an organization if all stakeholders are not consulted regarding Hybrid Solutions?
<--- Score

39. To whom do you add value?
<--- Score

40. Why not do Hybrid Solutions?
<--- Score

41. Are your responses positive or negative?
<--- Score

42. What are the long-term Hybrid Solutions goals?
<--- Score

43. Why should you adopt a Hybrid Solutions framework?

<--- Score

44. Who is responsible for Hybrid Solutions?

<--- Score

45. How do you lead with Hybrid Solutions in mind?

<--- Score

46. How will you know that the Hybrid Solutions project has been successful?

<--- Score

47. How do you create buy-in?

<--- Score

48. What you are going to do to affect the numbers?

<--- Score

49. Are assumptions made in Hybrid Solutions stated explicitly?

<--- Score

50. Do Hybrid Solutions rules make a reasonable demand on a users capabilities?

<--- Score

51. Will there be any necessary staff changes (redundancies or new hires)?

<--- Score

52. What one word do you want to own in the minds of your customers, employees, and partners?

<--- Score

53. Can you break it down?
<--- Score

54. Do you think Hybrid Solutions accomplishes the goals you expect it to accomplish?
<--- Score

55. How do you ensure that implementations of Hybrid Solutions products are done in a way that ensures safety?
<--- Score

56. How do you foster innovation?
<--- Score

57. Who else should you help?
<--- Score

58. How do customers see your organization?
<--- Score

59. Who are four people whose careers you have enhanced?
<--- Score

60. What happens at your organization when people fail?
<--- Score

61. Do you think you know, or do you know you know ?
<--- Score

62. What role does communication play in the success or failure of a Hybrid Solutions project?
<--- Score

63. Can you do all this work?
<--- Score

64. What are strategies for increasing support and reducing opposition?
<--- Score

65. What Hybrid Solutions modifications can you make work for you?
<--- Score

66. What have been your experiences in defining long range Hybrid Solutions goals?
<--- Score

67. Is the impact that Hybrid Solutions has shown?
<--- Score

68. How can you become the company that would put you out of business?
<--- Score

69. Can you maintain your growth without detracting from the factors that have contributed to your success?
<--- Score

70. What are your personal philosophies regarding Hybrid Solutions and how do they influence your work?
<--- Score

71. How long will it take to change?
<--- Score

72. How much contingency will be available in the budget?
<--- Score

73. In the past year, what have you done (or could you have done) to increase the accurate perception of your company/brand as ethical and honest?
<--- Score

74. Who is responsible for ensuring appropriate resources (time, people and money) are allocated to Hybrid Solutions?
<--- Score

75. What will be the consequences to the stakeholder (financial, reputation etc) if Hybrid Solutions does not go ahead or fails to deliver the objectives?
<--- Score

76. If your company went out of business tomorrow, would anyone who doesn't get a paycheck here care?
<--- Score

77. How do you transition from the baseline to the target?
<--- Score

78. What are your most important goals for the strategic Hybrid Solutions objectives?
<--- Score

79. Who is responsible for errors?
<--- Score

80. What is the recommended frequency of auditing?

<--- Score

81. If there were zero limitations, what would you do differently?
<--- Score

82. Are you maintaining a past–present–future perspective throughout the Hybrid Solutions discussion?
<--- Score

83. Is Hybrid Solutions realistic, or are you setting yourself up for failure?
<--- Score

84. Is a Hybrid Solutions team work effort in place?
<--- Score

85. What goals did you miss?
<--- Score

86. Why is it important to have senior management support for a Hybrid Solutions project?
<--- Score

87. Is maximizing Hybrid Solutions protection the same as minimizing Hybrid Solutions loss?
<--- Score

88. How do you keep the momentum going?
<--- Score

89. Which individuals, teams or departments will be involved in Hybrid Solutions?
<--- Score

90. What happens when a new employee joins the organization?
<--- Score

91. What threat is Hybrid Solutions addressing?
<--- Score

92. Who are the key stakeholders?
<--- Score

93. Do you have enough freaky customers in your portfolio pushing you to the limit day in and day out?
<--- Score

94. At what moment would you think; Will I get fired?
<--- Score

95. Who do we want your customers to become?
<--- Score

96. What happens if you do not have enough funding?
<--- Score

97. How likely is it that a customer would recommend your company to a friend or colleague?
<--- Score

98. Are you making progress, and are you making progress as Hybrid Solutions leaders?
<--- Score

99. How will you motivate the stakeholders with the least vested interest?
<--- Score

100. Are you satisfied with your current role? If not, what is missing from it?
<--- Score

101. What could happen if you do not do it?
<--- Score

102. How do you know if you are successful?
<--- Score

103. Are you using a design thinking approach and integrating Innovation, Hybrid Solutions Experience, and Brand Value?
<--- Score

104. What are the success criteria that will indicate that Hybrid Solutions objectives have been met and the benefits delivered?
<--- Score

105. Do you say no to customers for no reason?
<--- Score

106. How do you govern and fulfill your societal responsibilities?
<--- Score

107. What management system can you use to leverage the Hybrid Solutions experience, ideas, and concerns of the people closest to the work to be done?
<--- Score

108. Is it economical; do you have the time and money?

<--- Score

109. What is the overall talent health of your organization as a whole at senior levels, and for each organization reporting to a member of the Senior Leadership Team?
<--- Score

110. Is there any reason to believe the opposite of my current belief?
<--- Score

111. How do you set Hybrid Solutions stretch targets and how do you get people to not only participate in setting these stretch targets but also that they strive to achieve these?
<--- Score

112. Can the schedule be done in the given time?
<--- Score

113. Is a Hybrid Solutions breakthrough on the horizon?
<--- Score

114. What would have to be true for the option on the table to be the best possible choice?
<--- Score

115. Has implementation been effective in reaching specified objectives so far?
<--- Score

116. How do you keep records, of what?
<--- Score

117. What are you challenging?

<--- Score

118. Think of your Hybrid Solutions project, what are the main functions?

<--- Score

119. Is Hybrid Solutions dependent on the successful delivery of a current project?

<--- Score

120. If no one would ever find out about your accomplishments, how would you lead differently?

<--- Score

121. What are the key enablers to make this Hybrid Solutions move?

<--- Score

122. What are the gaps in your knowledge and experience?

<--- Score

123. Who uses your product in ways you never expected?

<--- Score

124. Do you have an implicit bias for capital investments over people investments?

<--- Score

125. What is your BATNA (best alternative to a negotiated agreement)?

<--- Score

126. How can you become more high-tech but still

be high touch?
<--- Score

127. Have benefits been optimized with all key stakeholders?
<--- Score

128. How does Hybrid Solutions integrate with other stakeholder initiatives?
<--- Score

129. Is there a work around that you can use?
<--- Score

130. What do we do when new problems arise?
<--- Score

131. Are there any activities that you can take off your to do list?
<--- Score

132. Who do you think the world wants your organization to be?
<--- Score

133. Why is Hybrid Solutions important for you now?
<--- Score

134. What are specific Hybrid Solutions rules to follow?
<--- Score

135. Where can you break convention?
<--- Score

136. What is effective Hybrid Solutions?

<--- Score

137. Who have you, as a company, historically been when you've been at your best?
<--- Score

138. What are you trying to prove to yourself, and how might it be hijacking your life and business success?
<--- Score

139. How do you make it meaningful in connecting Hybrid Solutions with what users do day-to-day?
<--- Score

140. How can you incorporate support to ensure safe and effective use of Hybrid Solutions into the services that you provide?
<--- Score

141. Do you have the right capabilities and capacities?
<--- Score

142. What is the range of capabilities?
<--- Score

143. What is the estimated value of the project?
<--- Score

144. What Hybrid Solutions skills are most important?
<--- Score

145. Who will be responsible for deciding whether Hybrid Solutions goes ahead or not after the initial investigations?

<--- Score

146. Why should people listen to you?
<--- Score

147. Are the assumptions believable and achievable?
<--- Score

148. Are you changing as fast as the world around you?
<--- Score

149. Is the Hybrid Solutions organization completing tasks effectively and efficiently?
<--- Score

150. What was the last experiment you ran?
<--- Score

151. Who will provide the final approval of Hybrid Solutions deliverables?
<--- Score

152. What business benefits will Hybrid Solutions goals deliver if achieved?
<--- Score

153. Have new benefits been realized?
<--- Score

154. What are the potential basics of Hybrid Solutions fraud?
<--- Score

155. How will you insure seamless interoperability of Hybrid Solutions moving forward?

<--- Score

156. How is implementation research currently incorporated into each of your goals?
<--- Score

157. What projects are going on in the organization today, and what resources are those projects using from the resource pools?
<--- Score

158. Would you rather sell to knowledgeable and informed customers or to uninformed customers?
<--- Score

159. How do you maintain Hybrid Solutions's Integrity?
<--- Score

160. How do you listen to customers to obtain actionable information?
<--- Score

161. Who will manage the integration of tools?
<--- Score

162. Do you know what you are doing? And who do you call if you don't?
<--- Score

163. Who is on the team?
<--- Score

164. Which Hybrid Solutions goals are the most important?
<--- Score

165. What are current Hybrid Solutions paradigms?
<--- Score

166. How do you determine the key elements that affect Hybrid Solutions workforce satisfaction, how are these elements determined for different workforce groups and segments?
<--- Score

167. What is it like to work for you?
<--- Score

168. How important is Hybrid Solutions to the user organizations mission?
<--- Score

169. How do you provide a safe environment -physically and emotionally?
<--- Score

170. Do you have the right people on the bus?
<--- Score

171. Operational - will it work?
<--- Score

172. What are the essentials of internal Hybrid Solutions management?
<--- Score

173. How much does Hybrid Solutions help?
<--- Score

174. What relationships among Hybrid Solutions trends do you perceive?

<--- Score

175. What stupid rule would you most like to kill?
<--- Score

176. How are you doing compared to your industry?
<--- Score

177. Do you know who is a friend or a foe?
<--- Score

178. Who, on the executive team or the board, has spoken to a customer recently?
<--- Score

179. If you had to rebuild your organization without any traditional competitive advantages (i.e., no killer technology, promising research, innovative product/ service delivery model, etcetera), how would your people have to approach their work and collaborate together in order to create the necessary conditions for success?
<--- Score

180. What would you recommend your friend do if he/she were facing this dilemma?
<--- Score

181. Will it be accepted by users?
<--- Score

182. What is an unauthorized commitment?
<--- Score

183. How do you engage the workforce, in addition to

satisfying them?
<--- Score

184. Why will customers want to buy your organizations products/services?
<--- Score

185. How do senior leaders deploy your organizations vision and values through your leadership system, to the workforce, to key suppliers and partners, and to customers and other stakeholders, as appropriate?
<--- Score

186. How can you negotiate Hybrid Solutions successfully with a stubborn boss, an irate client, or a deceitful coworker?
<--- Score

187. How do you deal with Hybrid Solutions changes?
<--- Score

188. If you find that you havent accomplished one of the goals for one of the steps of the Hybrid Solutions strategy, what will you do to fix it?
<--- Score

189. What is the source of the strategies for Hybrid Solutions strengthening and reform?
<--- Score

190. If you do not follow, then how to lead?
<--- Score

191. Were lessons learned captured and communicated?
<--- Score

192. What is the purpose of Hybrid Solutions in relation to the mission?
<--- Score

193. Do you have past Hybrid Solutions successes?
<--- Score

194. When information truly is ubiquitous, when reach and connectivity are completely global, when computing resources are infinite, and when a whole new set of impossibilities are not only possible, but happening, what will that do to your business?
<--- Score

195. What does your signature ensure?
<--- Score

196. What have you done to protect your business from competitive encroachment?
<--- Score

197. If you were responsible for initiating and implementing major changes in your organization, what steps might you take to ensure acceptance of those changes?
<--- Score

198. If you got fired and a new hire took your place, what would she do different?
<--- Score

199. How do you stay inspired?
<--- Score

200. Marketing budgets are tighter, consumers are

more skeptical, and social media has changed forever the way we talk about Hybrid Solutions, how do you gain traction?

<--- Score

201. What is the kind of project structure that would be appropriate for your Hybrid Solutions project, should it be formal and complex, or can it be less formal and relatively simple?

<--- Score

202. Whom among your colleagues do you trust, and for what?

<--- Score

203. How do you go about securing Hybrid Solutions?

<--- Score

204. What is the overall business strategy?

<--- Score

205. Are all key stakeholders present at all Structured Walkthroughs?

<--- Score

206. Is there any existing Hybrid Solutions governance structure?

<--- Score

207. What is something you believe that nearly no one agrees with you on?

<--- Score

208. How do you accomplish your long range Hybrid Solutions goals?

<--- Score

209. Are you paying enough attention to the partners your company depends on to succeed?
<--- Score

210. How do you foster the skills, knowledge, talents, attributes, and characteristics you want to have?
<--- Score

211. What is your formula for success in Hybrid Solutions ?
<--- Score

212. Do you see more potential in people than they do in themselves?
<--- Score

Add up total points for this section:
_ _ _ _ _ = Total points for this section

Divided by: _ _ _ _ _ _ (number of statements answered) = _ _ _ _ _ _
Average score for this section

Transfer your score to the Hybrid Solutions Index at the beginning of the Self-Assessment.

Hybrid Solutions and Managing Projects, Criteria for Project Managers:

1.0 Initiating Process Group: Hybrid Solutions

1. Does the Hybrid Solutions project team have enough people to execute the Hybrid Solutions project plan?

2. If action is called for, what form should it take?

3. What will be the pressing issues of tomorrow?

4. Who is funding the Hybrid Solutions project?

5. Mitigate. what will you do to minimize the impact should the risk event occur?

6. At which stage, in a typical Hybrid Solutions project do stake holders have maximum influence?

7. Were resources available as planned?

8. Information sharing?

9. How will you know you did it?

10. When must it be done?

11. What must be done?

12. Were decisions made in a timely manner?

13. Are there resources to maintain and support the outcome of the Hybrid Solutions project?

14. Are stakeholders properly informed about the

status of the Hybrid Solutions project?

15. How well did the chosen processes fit the needs of the Hybrid Solutions project?

16. Which of six sigmas dmaic phases focuses on the measurement of internal process that affect factors that are critical to quality?

17. What were things that you need to improve?

18. Have requirements been tested, approved, and fulfill the Hybrid Solutions project scope?

19. Did the Hybrid Solutions project team have the right skills?

1.1 Project Charter: Hybrid Solutions

20. Pop quiz – which are the same inputs as in the Hybrid Solutions project charter?

21. What are some examples of a business case?

22. Will this replace an existing product?

23. When is a charter needed?

24. Customer benefits: what customer requirements does this Hybrid Solutions project address?

25. What changes can you make to improve?

26. Why Outsource?

27. Are you building in-house ?

28. What is the purpose of the Hybrid Solutions project?

29. Success determination factors: how will the success of the Hybrid Solutions project be determined from the customers perspective?

30. Strategic fit: what is the strategic initiative identifier for this Hybrid Solutions project?

31. What metrics could you look at?

32. Assumptions: what factors, for planning purposes, are you considering to be true?

33. When do you use a Hybrid Solutions project Charter?

34. What barriers do you predict to your success?

35. When will this occur?

36. What outcome, in measureable terms, are you hoping to accomplish?

37. Why have you chosen the aim you have set forth?

38. Where and how does the team fit within your organization structure?

39. Run it as as a startup?

1.2 Stakeholder Register: Hybrid Solutions

40. What opportunities exist to provide communications?

41. What are the major Hybrid Solutions project milestones requiring communications or providing communications opportunities?

42. Is your organization ready for change?

43. How will reports be created?

44. How should employers make voices heard?

45. Who are the stakeholders?

46. How much influence do they have on the Hybrid Solutions project?

47. Who is managing stakeholder engagement?

48. Who wants to talk about Security?

49. How big is the gap?

50. What & Why?

51. What is the power of the stakeholder?

1.3 Stakeholder Analysis Matrix: Hybrid Solutions

52. New technologies, services, ideas?

53. Alliances: with which other actors is the actor allied, how are they interconnected?

54. Who has been involved in the area (thematic or geographic) in the past?

55. Who determines value?

56. Are there people who ise voices or interests in the issue may not be heard?

57. Which conditions out of the control of the management are crucial for the sustainability of its effects?

58. Morale, commitment, leadership?

59. Supporters; who are the supporters?

60. What is the stakeholders power and status in relation to the Hybrid Solutions project?

61. Innovative aspects?

62. What is your Advocacy Strategy?

63. Technology development and innovation?

64. What resources might the stakeholder bring to the Hybrid Solutions project?

65. Competitor intentions - various?

66. How does the Hybrid Solutions project involve consultations or collaboration with other organizations?

67. Arena: in what fields are the actors active, where are they present?

68. What do you Evaluate?

69. Is changing technology threatening your organizations position?

70. Who is most dependent on the resources at stake?

2.0 Planning Process Group: Hybrid Solutions

71. Who are the Hybrid Solutions project stakeholders?

72. What do they need to know about the Hybrid Solutions project?

73. What business situation is being addressed?

74. Does it make any difference if you are successful?

75. Is the Hybrid Solutions project making progress in helping to achieve the set results?

76. What is the NEXT thing to do?

77. How many days can task X be late in starting without affecting the Hybrid Solutions project completion date?

78. What type of estimation method are you using?

79. Professionals want to know what is expected from them; what are the deliverables?

80. Does the program have follow-up mechanisms (to verify the quality of the products, punctuality of delivery, etc.) to measure progress in the achievement of the envisaged results?

81. Are the necessary foundations in place to ensure

the sustainability of the results of the Hybrid Solutions project?

82. How does activity resource estimation affect activity duration estimation?

83. To what extent do the intervention objectives and strategies of the Hybrid Solutions project respond to your organizations plans?

84. What should you do next?

85. How can you make your needs known?

86. Just how important is your work to the overall success of the Hybrid Solutions project?

87. To what extent have the target population and participants made the activities own, taking an active role in it?

88. Have more efficient (sensitive) and appropriate measures been adopted to respond to the political and socio-cultural problems identified?

89. How can you tell when you are done?

90. The Hybrid Solutions project charter is created in which Hybrid Solutions project management process group?

2.1 Project Management Plan: Hybrid Solutions

91. Who manages integration?

92. How do you manage integration?

93. If the Hybrid Solutions project is complex or scope is specialized, do you have appropriate and/or qualified staff available to perform the tasks?

94. When is a Hybrid Solutions project management plan created?

95. What is the business need?

96. How do you manage time?

97. When is the Hybrid Solutions project management plan created?

98. Do there need to be organizational changes?

99. Is mitigation authorized or recommended?

100. Are comparable cost estimates used for comparing, screening and selecting alternative plans, and has a reasonable cost estimate been developed for the recommended plan?

101. Is the budget realistic?

102. What does management expect of PMs?

103. What went wrong?

104. What is Hybrid Solutions project scope management?

105. What is the justification?

106. Are calculations and results of analyzes essentially correct?

107. If the Hybrid Solutions project management plan is a comprehensive document that guides you in Hybrid Solutions project execution and control, then what should it NOT contain?

108. Does the implementation plan have an appropriate division of responsibilities?

109. Did the planning effort collaborate to develop solutions that integrate expertise, policies, programs, and Hybrid Solutions projects across entities?

110. Are there any client staffing expectations?

2.2 Scope Management Plan: Hybrid Solutions

111. Are internal Hybrid Solutions project status meetings held at reasonable intervals?

112. Do you keep stake holders informed?

113. Do Hybrid Solutions project managers participating in the Hybrid Solutions project know the Hybrid Solutions projects true status first hand?

114. Have Hybrid Solutions project team accountabilities & responsibilities been clearly defined?

115. Pop quiz – what changed on Hybrid Solutions project scope statement input?

116. What are the Quality Assurance overheads?

117. Are Hybrid Solutions project contact logs kept up to date?

118. Is there an on-going process in place to monitor Hybrid Solutions project risks?

119. Do you secure formal approval of changes and requirements from stakeholders?

120. Who is responsible for monitoring the Hybrid Solutions project scope to ensure the Hybrid Solutions project remains within the scope baseline?

121. Sensitivity analysis?

122. What is the estimated cost of creating and implementing?

123. Have Hybrid Solutions project management standards and procedures been identified / established and documented?

124. Is it possible to track all classes of Hybrid Solutions project work (e.g. scheduled, un-scheduled, defect repair, etc.)?

125. What problem is being solved by delivering this Hybrid Solutions project?

126. What should you drop in order to add something new?

127. Is it standard practice to formally commit stakeholders to the Hybrid Solutions project via agreements?

128. Has a structured approach been used to break work effort into manageable components (WBS)?

129. Pareto diagrams, statistical sampling, flow charting or trend analysis used quality monitoring?

2.3 Requirements Management Plan: Hybrid Solutions

130. How will requirements be managed?

131. Who has the authority to reject Hybrid Solutions project requirements?

132. How detailed should the Hybrid Solutions project get?

133. Did you avoid subjective, flowery or non-specific statements?

134. How will bidders price evaluations be done, by deliverables, phases, or in a big bang?

135. Do you know which stakeholders will participate in the requirements effort?

136. Is the user satisfied?

137. The wbs is developed as part of a joint planning session. and how do you know that youhave done this right?

138. Who will finally present the work or product(s) for acceptance?

139. Do you have price sheets and a methodology for determining the total proposal cost?

140. After the requirements are gathered and set

forth on the requirements register, theyre little more than a laundry list of items. Some may be duplicates, some might conflict with others and some will be too broad or too vague to understand. Describe how the requirements will be analyzed. Who will perform the analysis?

141. Did you distinguish the scope of work the contractor(s) will be required to do?

142. Describe the process for rejecting the Hybrid Solutions project requirements. Who has the authority to reject Hybrid Solutions project requirements?

143. How knowledgeable is the team in the proposed application area?

144. How often will the reporting occur?

145. How will unresolved questions be handled once approval has been obtained?

146. Do you expect stakeholders to be cooperative?

147. Will the contractors involved take full responsibility?

148. How knowledgeable is the primary Stakeholder(s) in the proposed application area?

2.4 Requirements Documentation: Hybrid Solutions

149. Where do you define what is a customer, what are the attributes of customer?

150. Do technical resources exist?

151. Can the requirement be changed without a large impact on other requirements?

152. The problem with gathering requirements is right there in the word gathering. What images does it conjure?

153. What are the acceptance criteria?

154. Does your organization restrict technical alternatives?

155. What marketing channels do you want to use: e-mail, letter or sms?

156. What is a show stopper in the requirements?

157. Is new technology needed?

158. How linear / iterative is your Requirements Gathering process (or will it be)?

159. Is the origin of the requirement clearly stated?

160. What is the risk associated with the technology?

161. What are the attributes of a customer?

162. How does what is being described meet the business need?

163. How does the proposed Hybrid Solutions project contribute to the overall objectives of your organization?

164. Consistency. are there any requirements conflicts?

165. What will be the integration problems?

166. How to document system requirements?

167. What are the potential disadvantages/ advantages?

168. What variations exist for a process?

2.5 Requirements Traceability Matrix: Hybrid Solutions

169. How small is small enough?

170. How will it affect the stakeholders personally in career?

171. What percentage of Hybrid Solutions projects are producing traceability matrices between requirements and other work products?

172. What are the chronologies, contingencies, consequences, criteria?

173. Will you use a Requirements Traceability Matrix?

174. How do you manage scope?

175. Is there a requirements traceability process in place?

176. What is the WBS?

177. Why do you manage scope?

178. Do you have a clear understanding of all subcontracts in place?

179. Why use a WBS?

180. Describe the process for approving requirements so they can be added to the traceability matrix and

Hybrid Solutions project work can be performed. Will the Hybrid Solutions project requirements become approved in writing?

2.6 Project Scope Statement: Hybrid Solutions

181. Were key Hybrid Solutions project stakeholders brought into the Hybrid Solutions project Plan?

182. Has everyone approved the Hybrid Solutions projects scope statement?

183. What is change?

184. Is your organization structure appropriate for the Hybrid Solutions projects size and complexity?

185. Will the Hybrid Solutions project risks be managed according to the Hybrid Solutions projects risk management process?

186. What are the major deliverables of the Hybrid Solutions project?

187. Did your Hybrid Solutions project ask for this?

188. Will all Hybrid Solutions project issues be unconditionally tracked through the issue resolution process?

189. Write a brief purpose statement for this Hybrid Solutions project. Include a business justification statement. What is the product of this Hybrid Solutions project?

190. Have you been able to thoroughly document

the Hybrid Solutions projects assumptions and constraints?

191. Will the qa related information be reported regularly as part of the status reporting mechanisms?

192. If there is an independent oversight contractor, have they signed off on the Hybrid Solutions project Plan?

193. Will the risk documents be filed?

194. Are there specific processes you will use to evaluate and approve/reject changes?

195. Elements that deal with providing the detail?

196. Were potential customers involved early in the planning process?

197. Is the Hybrid Solutions project organization documented and on file?

198. If you were to write a list of what should not be included in the scope statement, what are the things that you would recommend be described as out-of-scope?

199. Does the scope statement still need some clarity?

2.7 Assumption and Constraint Log: Hybrid Solutions

200. What do you log?

201. What worked well?

202. What weaknesses do you have?

203. How can constraints be violated?

204. If appropriate, is the deliverable content consistent with current Hybrid Solutions project documents and in compliance with the Document Management Plan?

205. How many Hybrid Solutions project staff does this specific process affect?

206. What is positive about the current process?

207. Do documented requirements exist for all critical components and areas, including technical, business, interfaces, performance, security and conversion requirements?

208. Is the steering committee active in Hybrid Solutions project oversight?

209. Is the amount of effort justified by the anticipated value of forming a new process?

210. What if failure during recovery?

211. Does the document/deliverable meet general requirements (for example, statement of work) for all deliverables?

212. Is the current scope of the Hybrid Solutions project substantially different than that originally defined in the approved Hybrid Solutions project plan?

213. What do you audit?

214. Is this process still needed?

215. Are there processes defining how software will be developed including development methods, overall timeline for development, software product standards, and traceability?

216. Has a Hybrid Solutions project Communications Plan been developed?

217. Does a specific action and/or state that is known to violate security policy occur?

218. Are there unnecessary steps that are creating bottlenecks and/or causing people to wait?

219. Is there documentation of system capability requirements, data requirements, environment requirements, security requirements, and computer and hardware requirements?

2.8 Work Breakdown Structure: Hybrid Solutions

220. Do you need another level?

221. When do you stop?

222. Who has to do it?

223. How far down?

224. How big is a work-package?

225. Is the work breakdown structure (wbs) defined and is the scope of the Hybrid Solutions project clear with assigned deliverable owners?

226. Where does it take place?

227. How will you and your Hybrid Solutions project team define the Hybrid Solutions projects scope and work breakdown structure?

228. What is the probability that the Hybrid Solutions project duration will exceed xx weeks?

229. Why is it useful?

230. What has to be done?

231. Why would you develop a Work Breakdown Structure?

232. Is it a change in scope?

233. When does it have to be done?

234. What is the probability of completing the Hybrid Solutions project in less that xx days?

235. Is it still viable?

236. How much detail?

2.9 WBS Dictionary: Hybrid Solutions

237. Are all authorized tasks assigned to identified organizational elements?

238. Are the bases and rates for allocating costs from each indirect pool to commercial work consistent with the already stated used to allocate corresponding costs to Government contracts?

239. Are records maintained to show full accountability for all material purchased for the contract, including the residual inventory?

240. Are indirect costs charged to the appropriate indirect pools and incurring organization?

241. Are the contractors estimates of costs at completion reconcilable with cost data reported to us?

242. The already stated responsible for overhead performance control of related costs?

243. Are retroactive changes to budgets for completed work specifically prohibited in an established procedure, and is this procedure adhered to?

244. Are the overhead pools formally and adequately identified?

245. The Hybrid Solutions projected business base for each period?

246. Does the contractors system provide unit or lot costs when applicable?

247. Is all budget available as management reserve identified and excluded from the performance measurement baseline?

248. Evaluate the performance of operating organizations?

249. Are procedures established to prevent changes to the contract budget base other than the already stated authorized by contractual action?

250. Budgets assigned to control accounts?

251. Contemplated overhead expenditure for each period based on the best information currently available?

252. Wbs elements contractually specified for reporting of status to you (lowest level only)?

253. Are overhead budgets and costs being handled according to the disclosure statement when applicable, or otherwise properly classified (for example, engineering overhead, IR&D)?

254. Incurrence of actual indirect costs in excess of budgets, by element of expense?

255. Does the contractors system provide for accurate cost accumulation and assignment to control accounts in a manner consistent with the budgets using recognized acceptable costing techniques?

2.10 Schedule Management Plan: Hybrid Solutions

256. What happens if a warning is triggered?

257. What is the difference between % Complete and % work?

258. Are target dates established for each milestone deliverable?

259. Identify the amount of schedule variation that triggers a warning. What happens if a warning is triggered?

260. Is the assigned Hybrid Solutions project manager a PMP (Certified Hybrid Solutions project manager) and experienced?

261. Is there an approved case?

262. List all schedule constraints here. Must the Hybrid Solutions project be complete by a specified date?

263. Have reserves been created to address risks?

264. Have the key functions and capabilities been defined and assigned to each release or iteration?

265. Does all Hybrid Solutions project documentation reside in a common repository for easy access?

266. Has your organization readiness assessment

been conducted?

267. Personnel with expertise?

268. Quality assurance overheads?

269. Are non-critical path items updated and agreed upon with the teams?

270. Is an industry recognized mechanized support tool(s) being used for Hybrid Solutions project scheduling & tracking?

271. Does the ims include all contract and/or designated management control milestones?

272. Are meeting objectives identified for each meeting?

273. Is the ims development and management approach described?

274. Are tasks tracked by hours?

275. Was your organizations estimating methodology being used and followed?

2.11 Activity List: Hybrid Solutions

276. What will be performed?

277. When do the individual activities need to start and finish?

278. What went right?

279. How detailed should a Hybrid Solutions project get?

280. How difficult will it be to do specific activities on this Hybrid Solutions project?

281. Should you include sub-activities?

282. How much slack is available in the Hybrid Solutions project?

283. Can you determine the activity that must finish, before this activity can start?

284. For other activities, how much delay can be tolerated?

285. What did not go as well?

286. What is the probability the Hybrid Solutions project can be completed in xx weeks?

287. When will the work be performed?

288. Who will perform the work?

289. How should ongoing costs be monitored to try to keep the Hybrid Solutions project within budget?

290. Are the required resources available or need to be acquired?

291. What is your organizations history in doing similar activities?

292. What are you counting on?

293. What are the critical bottleneck activities?

294. What went well?

295. How will it be performed?

2.12 Activity Attributes: Hybrid Solutions

296. How else could the items be grouped?

297. Do you feel very comfortable with your prediction?

298. How difficult will it be to complete specific activities on this Hybrid Solutions project?

299. Is there a trend during the year?

300. Were there other ways you could have organized the data to achieve similar results?

301. What is the general pattern here?

302. Can you re-assign any activities to another resource to resolve an over-allocation?

303. How many days do you need to complete the work scope with a limit of X number of resources?

304. Have constraints been applied to the start and finish milestones for the phases?

305. How many resources do you need to complete the work scope within a limit of X number of days?

306. Activity: what is Missing?

307. Can more resources be added?

308. What activity do you think you should spend the most time on?

309. Would you consider either of corresponding activities an outlier?

310. Is there anything planned that does not need to be here?

311. What is missing?

312. Where else does it apply?

313. Are the required resources available?

314. Have you identified the Activity Leveling Priority code value on each activity?

315. Does your organization of the data change its meaning?

2.13 Milestone List: Hybrid Solutions

316. Continuity, supply chain robustness?

317. How late can the activity start?

318. Sustaining internal capabilities?

319. Information and research?

320. Reliability of data, plan predictability?

321. Insurmountable weaknesses?

322. Environmental effects?

323. Level of the Innovation?

324. Sustainable financial backing?

325. Loss of key staff?

326. Legislative effects?

327. What date will the task finish?

328. Who will manage the Hybrid Solutions project on a day-to-day basis?

329. How late can the activity finish?

330. What specific improvements did you make to the Hybrid Solutions project proposal since the previous time?

331. Usps (unique selling points)?

332. Milestone pages should display the UserID of the person who added the milestone. Does a report or query exist that provides this audit information?

333. What would happen if a delivery of material was one week late?

2.14 Network Diagram: Hybrid Solutions

334. What is the lowest cost to complete this Hybrid Solutions project in xx weeks?

335. What job or jobs follow it?

336. If x is long, what would be the completion time if you break x into two parallel parts of y weeks and z weeks?

337. What job or jobs could run concurrently?

338. What controls the start and finish of a job?

339. If a current contract exists, can you provide the vendor name, contract start, and contract expiration date?

340. What activity must be completed immediately before this activity can start?

341. Which type of network diagram allows you to depict four types of dependencies?

342. What activities must occur simultaneously with this activity?

343. What job or jobs precede it?

344. Will crashing x weeks return more in benefits than it costs?

345. Can you calculate the confidence level?

346. Why must you schedule milestones, such as reviews, throughout the Hybrid Solutions project?

347. Where do you schedule uncertainty time?

348. What must be completed before an activity can be started?

349. Are you on time?

350. How difficult will it be to do specific activities on this Hybrid Solutions project?

2.15 Activity Resource Requirements: Hybrid Solutions

351. Time for overtime?

352. Do you use tools like decomposition and rolling-wave planning to produce the activity list and other outputs?

353. How do you handle petty cash?

354. Organizational Applicability?

355. When does monitoring begin?

356. Other support in specific areas?

357. How many signatures do you require on a check and does this match what is in your policy and procedures?

358. What is the Work Plan Standard?

359. Anything else?

360. Which logical relationship does the PDM use most often?

361. What are constraints that you might find during the Human Resource Planning process?

362. Are there unresolved issues that need to be addressed?

363. Why do you do that?

2.16 Resource Breakdown Structure: Hybrid Solutions

364. Why time management?

365. What are the requirements for resource data?

366. Who will use the system?

367. When do they need the information?

368. What defines a successful Hybrid Solutions project?

369. What is each stakeholders desired outcome for the Hybrid Solutions project?

370. What is Hybrid Solutions project communication management?

371. How can this help you with team building?

372. Who needs what information?

373. Why is this important?

374. What can you do to improve productivity?

375. What is the purpose of assigning and documenting responsibility?

376. Why do you do it?

377. What is the primary purpose of the human resource plan?

378. Who is allowed to perform which functions?

379. Goals for the Hybrid Solutions project. What is each stakeholders desired outcome for the Hybrid Solutions project?

380. Changes based on input from stakeholders?

2.17 Activity Duration Estimates: Hybrid Solutions

381. Briefly describe some key events in the history of Hybrid Solutions project management. What Hybrid Solutions project was the first to use modern Hybrid Solutions project management?

382. What type of information goes in a quality assurance plan?

383. List five reasons why organizations outsource. Why is there a growing trend in outsourcing, especially in the government?

384. Which suggestions do you find most useful?

385. Are Hybrid Solutions project activities decomposed into manageable components to ensure expected management control?

386. Consider the history of modern quality management. How have experts such as Deming, Juran, Crosby, and Taguchi affected the quality movement and todays use of Six Sigma?

387. Do you agree with the suggestions provided for improving Hybrid Solutions project communications?

388. Research recruiting and retention strategies at three different companies. What distinguishes one organization from another in this area?

389. Do checklists exist that list frequently performed activities?

390. Do they make sense?

391. Is a formal written notice that the contract is complete provided to the seller?

392. When a risk event occurs, is the risk response evaluated and the appropriate response implemented?

393. Are procedures defined by which the Hybrid Solutions project scope may be changed?

394. What is the difference between using brainstorming and the Delphi technique for risk identification?

395. Do stakeholders follow a procedure for formally accepting the Hybrid Solutions project scope?

396. Hybrid Solutions project manager is using weighted average duration estimates to perform schedule network analysis. Which type of mathematical analysis is being used?

397. Given your research into similar classes and the work you think is required for this Hybrid Solutions project, what assumptions, variables, or costs would you change from the information provided above?

398. Are risks that are likely to affect the Hybrid Solutions project identified and documented?

399. What are the main types of contracts if you do

decide to outsource?

2.18 Duration Estimating Worksheet: Hybrid Solutions

400. What is an Average Hybrid Solutions project?

401. Does the Hybrid Solutions project provide innovative ways for stakeholders to overcome obstacles or deliver better outcomes?

402. Why estimate costs?

403. Value pocket identification & quantification what are value pockets?

404. What info is needed?

405. Science = process: remember the scientific method?

406. When, then?

407. Is the Hybrid Solutions project responsive to community need?

408. Why estimate time and cost?

409. Done before proceeding with this activity or what can be done concurrently?

410. What is next?

411. Do any colleagues have experience with your organization and/or RFPs?

412. Is a construction detail attached (to aid in explanation)?

413. Small or large Hybrid Solutions project?

414. What is your role?

415. Is this operation cost effective?

2.19 Project Schedule: Hybrid Solutions

416. Why do you need to manage Hybrid Solutions project Risk?

417. How much slack is available in the Hybrid Solutions project?

418. Are activities connected because logic dictates the order in which others occur?

419. Are you working on the right risks?

420. Is Hybrid Solutions project work proceeding in accordance with the original Hybrid Solutions project schedule?

421. Did the final product meet or exceed user expectations?

422. How do you use schedules?

423. Why do you think schedule issues often cause the most conflicts on Hybrid Solutions projects?

424. Have all Hybrid Solutions project delays been adequately accounted for, communicated to all stakeholders and adjustments made in overall Hybrid Solutions project schedule?

425. Month Hybrid Solutions project take?

426. What is the most mis-scheduled part of process?

427. Meet requirements?

428. To what degree is do you feel the entire team was committed to the Hybrid Solutions project schedule?

429. Are the original Hybrid Solutions project schedule and budget realistic?

430. How do you know that youhave done this right?

431. How can you fix it?

432. How can you address that situation?

433. Understand the constraints used in preparing the schedule. Are activities connected because logic dictates the order in which others occur?

2.20 Cost Management Plan: Hybrid Solutions

434. If you sold 10x widgets on a day, what would the affect on costs be?

435. Was the scope definition used in task sequencing?

436. Hybrid Solutions project Objectives?

437. Is there a Steering Committee in place?

438. Is it possible to track all classes of Hybrid Solutions project work (e.g. scheduled, un-scheduled, defect repair, etc.)?

439. Cost management – how will the cost of changes be estimated and controlled?

440. Are Hybrid Solutions project team members committed fulltime?

441. Does the Hybrid Solutions project have a formal Hybrid Solutions project Charter?

442. Have all documents been archived in a Hybrid Solutions project repository for each release?

443. Are meeting minutes captured and sent out after the meeting?

444. Is the quality assurance team identified?

445. Do Hybrid Solutions project managers participating in the Hybrid Solutions project know the Hybrid Solutions projects true status first hand?

446. Has a resource management plan been created?

447. Is the schedule updated on a periodic basis?

448. Progress measurement and control – How will the Hybrid Solutions project measure and control progress?

449. Are procurement deliverables arriving on time and to specification?

450. What would you do differently what did not work?

451. Vac -variance at completion, how much over/under budget do you expect to be?

452. Has the budget been baselined?

2.21 Activity Cost Estimates: Hybrid Solutions

453. What were things that you did well, and could improve, and how?

454. What defines a successful Hybrid Solutions project?

455. Is there anything unique in this Hybrid Solutions projects scope statement that will affect resources?

456. What procedures are put in place regarding bidding and cost comparisons, if any?

457. Measurable - are the targets measurable?

458. Review – what are some common errors in activities to avoid?

459. How and when do you enter into Hybrid Solutions project Procurement Management?

460. Did the consultant work with local staff to develop local capacity?

461. Can you delete activities or make them inactive?

462. What skill level is required to do the job?

463. How do you fund change orders?

464. How do you change activities?

465. When do you enter into PPM?

466. What makes a good activity description?

467. Maintenance Reserve?

468. What is the activity inventory?

469. Is costing method consistent with study goals?

470. Can you change your activities?

2.22 Cost Estimating Worksheet: Hybrid Solutions

471. What is the estimated labor cost today based upon this information?

472. What happens to any remaining funds not used?

473. What can be included?

474. Ask: are others positioned to know, are others credible, and will others cooperate?

475. Identify the timeframe necessary to monitor progress and collect data to determine how the selected measure has changed?

476. Who is best positioned to know and assist in identifying corresponding factors?

477. Is the Hybrid Solutions project responsive to community need?

478. What is the purpose of estimating?

479. What costs are to be estimated?

480. Is it feasible to establish a control group arrangement?

481. What will others want?

482. Does the Hybrid Solutions project provide

innovative ways for stakeholders to overcome obstacles or deliver better outcomes?

483. What additional Hybrid Solutions project(s) could be initiated as a result of this Hybrid Solutions project?

484. Will the Hybrid Solutions project collaborate with the local community and leverage resources?

485. How will the results be shared and to whom?

486. Can a trend be established from historical performance data on the selected measure and are the criteria for using trend analysis or forecasting methods met?

2.23 Cost Baseline: Hybrid Solutions

487. Have the lessons learned been filed with the Hybrid Solutions project Management Office?

488. Is there anything unique in this Hybrid Solutions projects scope statement that will affect resources?

489. Have the resources used by the Hybrid Solutions project been reassigned to other units or Hybrid Solutions projects?

490. How likely is it to go wrong?

491. How long are you willing to wait before you find out were late?

492. Is the cr within Hybrid Solutions project scope?

493. Are there contingencies or conditions related to the acceptance?

494. Does the suggested change request seem to represent a necessary enhancement to the product?

495. What is the reality?

496. What is the consequence?

497. On time?

498. Who will use corresponding metrics ?

499. How do you manage cost?

500. Is there anything you need from upper management in order to be successful?

501. How accurate do cost estimates need to be?

502. What is the most important thing to do next to make your Hybrid Solutions project successful?

503. Has the documentation relating to operation and maintenance of the product(s) or service(s) been delivered to, and accepted by, operations management?

504. Is the requested change request a result of changes in other Hybrid Solutions project(s)?

2.24 Quality Management Plan: Hybrid Solutions

505. Are formal code reviews conducted?

506. How do you document and correct nonconformances?

507. How is equipment calibrated?

508. Sampling part of task?

509. How are changes approved?

510. How are new requirements or changes to requirements identified?

511. Who is responsible for writing the qapp?

512. How are deviations from procedures handled?

513. Are you following the quality standards?

514. What other teams / processes would be impacted by changes to the current process, and how?

515. How do you ensure that your sampling methods and procedures meet your data needs?

516. Have adequate resources been provided by management to ensure Hybrid Solutions project success?

517. Are there ways to reduce the time it takes to get something approved?

518. What data do you gather/use/compile?

519. Was trending evident between reviews?

520. What are your key performance measures/ indicators for tracking progress relative to your action plans?

521. Is staff trained on the software technologies that are being used on the Hybrid Solutions project?

2.25 Quality Metrics: Hybrid Solutions

522. What happens if you get an abnormal result?

523. What are you trying to accomplish?

524. Has risk analysis been adequately reviewed?

525. What metrics are important and most beneficial to measure?

526. Should a modifier be included?

527. What can manufacturing professionals do to ensure quality is seen as an integral part of the entire product lifecycle?

528. Are quality metrics defined?

529. If the defect rate during testing is substantially higher than that of the previous release (or a similar product), then ask: Did you plan for and actually improve testing effectiveness?

530. What are your organizations expectations for its quality Hybrid Solutions project?

531. How do you measure?

532. How can the effectiveness of each of the activities be measured?

533. Where is quality now?

534. What do you measure?

535. What if the biggest risk to your business were the already stated people who do not complain?

536. Have risk areas been identified?

537. When is the security analysis testing complete?

538. How should customers provide input?

539. What method of measurement do you use?

540. Do you stratify metrics by product or site?

2.26 Process Improvement Plan: Hybrid Solutions

541. What personnel are the sponsors for that initiative?

542. The motive is determined by asking, Why do you want to achieve this goal?

543. Does explicit definition of the measures exist?

544. What makes people good SPI coaches?

545. Modeling current processes is great, and will you ever see a return on that investment?

546. What actions are needed to address the problems and achieve the goals?

547. Have the frequency of collection and the points in the process where measurements will be made been determined?

548. Why quality management?

549. Where do you focus?

550. Where do you want to be?

551. Who should prepare the process improvement action plan?

552. Everyone agrees on what process improvement

is, right?

553. Does your process ensure quality?

554. What lessons have you learned so far?

555. Are you meeting the quality standards?

556. What personnel are the champions for the initiative?

557. Where are you now?

2.27 Responsibility Assignment Matrix: Hybrid Solutions

558. What are the constraints?

559. What are the known stakeholder requirements?

560. Performance to date and material commitment?

561. How many hours by each staff member/rate?

562. Does a missing responsibility indicate that the current Hybrid Solutions project is not yet fully understood?

563. Are the actual costs used for variance analysis reconcilable with data from the accounting system?

564. Who is going to do that work?

565. Do others have the time to dedicate to your Hybrid Solutions project?

566. Are people encouraged to bring up issues?

567. What simple tool can you use to help identify and prioritize Hybrid Solutions project risks that is very low tech and high touch?

568. Are there any drawbacks to using a responsibility assignment matrix?

569. Is work progressively subdivided into detailed

work packages as requirements are defined?

570. Availability – will the group or the person be available within the necessary time interval?

571. Does the contractor use objective results, design reviews and tests to trace schedule performance?

572. If a role has only Signing-off, or only Communicating responsibility and has no Performing, Accountable, or Monitoring responsibility, is it necessary?

573. Do you need to convince people that its well worth the time and effort?

574. How many people do you need?

575. Why cost benefit analysis?

2.28 Roles and Responsibilities: Hybrid Solutions

576. Are governance roles and responsibilities documented?

577. Are your policies supportive of a culture of quality data?

578. Are Hybrid Solutions project team roles and responsibilities identified and documented?

579. Key conclusions and recommendations: Are conclusions and recommendations relevant and acceptable?

580. What should you do now to prepare for your career 5+ years from now?

581. Attainable / achievable: the goal is attainable; can you actually accomplish the goal?

582. Was the expectation clearly communicated?

583. How well did the Hybrid Solutions project Team understand the expectations of specific roles and responsibilities?

584. Who: who is involved?

585. What specific behaviors did you observe?

586. Do the values and practices inherent in the

culture of your organization foster or hinder the process?

587. What is working well within your organizations performance management system?

588. Influence: what areas of organizational decision making are you able to influence when you do not have authority to make the final decision?

589. What areas would you highlight for changes or improvements?

590. Authority: what areas/Hybrid Solutions projects in your work do you have the authority to decide upon and act on the already stated decisions?

591. To decide whether to use a quality measurement, ask how will you know when it is achieved?

592. What is working well?

593. Where are you most strong as a supervisor?

594. Do you take the time to clearly define roles and responsibilities on Hybrid Solutions project tasks?

2.29 Human Resource Management Plan: Hybrid Solutions

595. Are the people assigned to the Hybrid Solutions project sufficiently qualified?

596. Are key risk mitigation strategies added to the Hybrid Solutions project schedule?

597. Have the procedures for identifying budget variances been followed?

598. Are vendor invoices audited for accuracy before payment?

599. What talent is needed?

600. Does the Hybrid Solutions project have a Quality Culture?

601. Are updated Hybrid Solutions project time & resource estimates reasonable based on the current Hybrid Solutions project stage?

602. Have all unresolved risks been documented?

603. Are estimating assumptions and constraints captured?

604. How will the Hybrid Solutions project manage expectations & meet needs and requirements?

605. List roles. what commitments have been made?

606. How to convince to employees that it is a necessary process?

607. Are adequate resources provided for the quality assurance function?

608. Is there an issues management plan in place?

609. Have activity relationships and interdependencies within tasks been adequately identified?

2.30 Communications Management Plan: Hybrid Solutions

610. Which stakeholders can influence others?

611. What data is going to be required?

612. Is the stakeholder role recognized by your organization?

613. Who will use or be affected by the result of a Hybrid Solutions project?

614. Do you then often overlook a key stakeholder or stakeholder group?

615. What approaches do you use?

616. What approaches to you feel are the best ones to use?

617. Are there common objectives between the team and the stakeholder?

618. What to know?

619. Why is stakeholder engagement important?

620. Why do you manage communications?

621. Conflict resolution -which method when?

622. How much time does it take to do it?

623. In your work, how much time is spent on stakeholder identification?

624. How were corresponding initiatives successful?

625. How did the term stakeholder originate?

626. Who is responsible?

627. Are the stakeholders getting the information others need, are others consulted, are concerns addressed?

628. Who is the stakeholder?

629. Do you prepare stakeholder engagement plans?

2.31 Risk Management Plan: Hybrid Solutions

630. Are the reports useful and easy to read?

631. Is a software Hybrid Solutions project management tool available?

632. What is the probability the risk avoidance strategy will be successful?

633. Is the necessary data being captured and is it complete and accurate?

634. How much risk can you tolerate?

635. If you can not fix it, how do you do it differently?

636. What things are likely to change?

637. What things might go wrong?

638. How risk averse are you?

639. What would you do?

640. Is security a central objective?

641. Degree of confidence in estimated size estimate?

642. How quickly does each item need to be resolved?

643. Is this an issue, action item, question or a risk?

644. Are formal technical reviews part of this process?

645. Have you worked with the customer in the past?

646. Does the Hybrid Solutions project have the authority and ability to avoid the risk?

647. How can the process be made more effective or less cumbersome (process improvements)?

648. What risks are tracked?

649. Are staff committed for the duration of the product?

2.32 Risk Register: Hybrid Solutions

650. Preventative actions - planned actions to reduce the likelihood a risk will occur and/or reduce the seriousness should it occur. What should you do now?

651. Assume the event happens, what is the Most Likely impact?

652. Who is accountable?

653. Who is going to do it?

654. What should you do now?

655. Do you require further engagement?

656. What can be done about it?

657. How often will the Risk Management Plan and Risk Register be formally reviewed, and by whom?

658. What is the appropriate level of risk management for this Hybrid Solutions project?

659. Recovery actions - planned actions taken once a risk has occurred to allow you to move on. What should you do after?

660. When is it going to be done?

661. Risk documentation: what reporting formats and processes will be used for risk management activities?

662. Schedule impact/severity estimated range (workdays) assume the event happens, what is the potential impact?

663. Is further information required before making a decision?

664. User involvement: do you have the right users?

665. What risks might negatively or positively affect achieving the Hybrid Solutions project objectives?

666. Methodology: how will risk management be performed on this Hybrid Solutions project?

667. What evidence do you have to justify the likelihood score of the risk (audit, incident report, claim, complaints, inspection, internal review)?

668. What will be done?

2.33 Probability and Impact Assessment: Hybrid Solutions

669. Do you have a mechanism for managing change?

670. Are testing tools available and suitable?

671. How realistic is the timing of introduction?

672. Have decisions that should be left open because of inadequate information on technology been identified and responsibility assigned for reducing the uncertainty?

673. Will new information become available during the Hybrid Solutions project?

674. Costs associated with late delivery or a defective product?

675. Are there any Hybrid Solutions projects similar to this one in existence?

676. Do you have specific methods that you use for each phase of the process?

677. What is the Hybrid Solutions project managers level of commitment and professionalism?

678. What can you do about it?

679. Are the best people available?

680. How is risk handled within this Hybrid Solutions project organization?

681. Are there new risks that mitigation strategies might introduce?

682. What are its business ethics?

683. Are staff committed for the duration of the Hybrid Solutions project?

684. Is a software Hybrid Solutions project management tool available?

685. Do the requirements require the creation of new algorithms?

686. What is the likelihood of a breakthrough?

687. How are you working with risks?

688. Are there alternative opinions/solutions/ processes you should explore?

2.34 Probability and Impact Matrix: Hybrid Solutions

689. Mandated delivery date?

690. Could others have been better mitigated?

691. What will be the likely political environment during the life of the Hybrid Solutions project?

692. Maximize short-term return on investment?

693. Are compilers and code generators available and suitable for the product to be built?

694. Is there any sign of biased ranking?

695. Does the customer understand the software process?

696. Do you know the order of planning yet?

697. What are the methods to deal with risks?

698. What are the chances the event will occur?

699. What has the Hybrid Solutions project manager forgotten to do?

700. What is Hybrid Solutions project risk management?

701. To what extent is the chosen technology

maturing?

702. How much is the probability of the risk occurring?

703. Risk categorization -which of your categories has more risk than others?

704. Which is an input to the risk management process?

705. Number of users of the product?

706. What are the chances the risk events will occur?

707. How can you understand and diagnose risks and identify sources?

2.35 Risk Data Sheet: Hybrid Solutions

708. Whom do you serve (customers)?

709. Will revised controls lead to tolerable risk levels?

710. What can happen?

711. What was measured?

712. What are you trying to achieve (Objectives)?

713. What is the chance that it will happen?

714. What will be the consequences if it happens?

715. Risk of what?

716. How do you handle product safely?

717. If it happens, what are the consequences?

718. What do you know?

719. What actions can be taken to eliminate or remove risk?

720. What are your core values?

721. Has a sensitivity analysis been carried out?

722. Potential for recurrence?

723. How can it happen?

724. What if client refuses?

2.36 Procurement Management Plan: Hybrid Solutions

725. Are milestone deliverables effectively tracked and compared to Hybrid Solutions project plan?

726. Hybrid Solutions project Objectives?

727. Are decisions made in a timely manner?

728. Are enough systems & user personnel assigned to the Hybrid Solutions project?

729. Are written status reports provided on a designated frequent basis?

730. Were escalated issues resolved promptly?

731. What are things that you need to improve?

732. Published materials?

733. What types of contracts will be used?

734. Are the results of quality assurance reviews provided to affected groups & individuals?

735. Are the key elements of a Hybrid Solutions project Charter present?

736. Is pert / critical path or equivalent methodology being used?

737. What areas are overlooked on this Hybrid Solutions project?

738. Are the Hybrid Solutions project plans updated on a frequent basis?

2.37 Source Selection Criteria: Hybrid Solutions

739. What documentation is necessary regarding electronic communications?

740. What information may not be provided?

741. What are the special considerations for preaward debriefings?

742. What should be the contracting officers strategy?

743. Does your documentation identify why the team concurs or differs with reported performance from past performance report (CPARs, questionnaire responses, etc.)?

744. In order of importance, which evaluation criteria are the most critical to the determination of your overall rating?

745. Who is on the Source Selection Advisory Committee?

746. Who must be notified?

747. Do you want to have them collaborate at subfactor level?

748. Is experience evaluated?

749. How are oral presentations documented?

750. What will you use to capture evaluation and subsequent documentation?

751. Is the contracting office likely to receive more purchase requests for this item or service during the coming year?

752. What is the role of counsel in the procurement process?

753. How should oral presentations be evaluated?

754. How do you facilitate evaluation against published criteria?

755. Can you prevent comparison of proposals?

756. When must you conduct a debriefing?

757. What benefits are accrued from issuing a DRFP in advance of issuing a final RFP?

758. How do you encourage efficiency and consistency?

2.38 Stakeholder Management Plan: Hybrid Solutions

759. Are there nonconformance issues?

760. Is the assigned Hybrid Solutions project manager a PMP (Certified Hybrid Solutions project manager) and experienced?

761. What are reporting requirements?

762. Does the Hybrid Solutions project have a Statement of Work?

763. Are there standards for code development?

764. Are metrics used to evaluate and manage Vendors?

765. Are the payment terms being followed?

766. What action will be taken once reports have been received?

767. Is there general agreement & acceptance of the current status and progress of the Hybrid Solutions project?

768. How will you engage this stakeholder and gain commitment?

769. Who is responsible for accepting the reports produced by the process?

770. Are the schedule estimates reasonable given the Hybrid Solutions project?

771. Have all documents been archived in a Hybrid Solutions project repository for each release?

772. What procedures will be utilised to ensure effective monitoring of Hybrid Solutions project progress?

773. Can the requirements be traced to the appropriate components of the solution, as well as test scripts?

774. Have all involved Hybrid Solutions project stakeholders and work groups committed to the Hybrid Solutions project?

2.39 Change Management Plan: Hybrid Solutions

775. What do you expect the target audience to do, say, think or feel as a result of this communication?

776. What did the people around you say about it?

777. What are the essentials of the message?

778. How might they respond to the message and if the response may be negative or open to misinterpretation, what else needs to be said?

779. What relationships will change?

780. How does the principle of senders and receivers make the Hybrid Solutions project communications effort more complex?

781. Has a training need analysis been carried out?

782. What risks may occur upfront?

783. What tasks are needed?

784. How will you deal with anger about the restricting of communications due to confidentiality considerations?

785. Which relationships will change?

786. Has this been negotiated with the customer and

sponsor?

787. What method and medium would you use to announce a message?

788. Would you need to tailor a special message for each segment of the audience?

789. What are the specific target groups/audiences that will be impacted by this change?

790. What are the responsibilities assigned to each role?

791. Is there a support model for this application and are the details available for distribution?

792. Who will be the change levers?

793. Who should be involved in developing a change management strategy?

794. What will be the preferred method of delivery?

3.0 Executing Process Group: Hybrid Solutions

795. What are the typical Hybrid Solutions project management skills?

796. What factors are contributing to progress or delay in the achievement of products and results?

797. How well did the chosen processes produce the expected results?

798. Do Hybrid Solutions project managers understand your organizational context for Hybrid Solutions projects?

799. Is the schedule for the set products being met?

800. What type of information goes in the quality assurance plan?

801. Would you rate yourself as being risk-averse, risk-neutral, or risk-seeking?

802. How can software assist in Hybrid Solutions project communications?

803. How well defined and documented were the Hybrid Solutions project management processes you chose to use?

804. How does Hybrid Solutions project management relate to other disciplines?

805. Who are the Hybrid Solutions project stakeholders?

806. How can your organization use a weighted decision matrix to evaluate proposals as part of source selection?

807. How does the job market and current state of the economy affect human resource management?

808. What does it mean to take a systems view of a Hybrid Solutions project?

809. What type of people would you want on your team?

810. What were things that you did very well and want to do the same again on the next Hybrid Solutions project?

811. What Hybrid Solutions projects and services are in the portfolio of your organization?

3.1 Team Member Status Report: Hybrid Solutions

812. How can you make it practical?

813. Are your organizations Hybrid Solutions projects more successful over time?

814. Does every department have to have a Hybrid Solutions project Manager on staff?

815. Do you have an Enterprise Hybrid Solutions project Management Office (EPMO)?

816. Does the product, good, or service already exist within your organization?

817. Does your organization have the means (staff, money, contract, etc.) to produce or to acquire the product, good, or service?

818. Are the attitudes of staff regarding Hybrid Solutions project work improving?

819. What is to be done?

820. Why is it to be done?

821. How does this product, good, or service meet the needs of the Hybrid Solutions project and your organization as a whole?

822. Will the staff do training or is that done by a third

party?

823. Is there evidence that staff is taking a more professional approach toward management of your organizations Hybrid Solutions projects?

824. What specific interest groups do you have in place?

825. When a teams productivity and success depend on collaboration and the efficient flow of information, what generally fails them?

826. Are the products of your organizations Hybrid Solutions projects meeting customers objectives?

827. How much risk is involved?

828. How will resource planning be done?

829. The problem with Reward & Recognition Programs is that the truly deserving people all too often get left out. How can you make it practical?

830. How it is to be done?

3.2 Change Request: Hybrid Solutions

831. Will new change requests be acknowledged in a timely manner?

832. What are the requirements for urgent changes?

833. Will this change conflict with other requirements changes (e.g., lead to conflicting operational scenarios)?

834. Should staff call into the helpdesk or go to the website?

835. Who is included in the change control team?

836. Has a formal technical review been conducted to assess technical correctness?

837. Who needs to approve change requests?

838. How many lines of code must be changed to implement the change?

839. Who can suggest changes?

840. Should a more thorough impact analysis be conducted?

841. Can you answer what happened, who did it, when did it happen, and what else will be affected?

842. Have scm procedures for noting the change, recording it, and reporting it been followed?

843. When do you create a change request?

844. How does your organization control changes before and after software is released to a customer?

845. What is the relationship between requirements attributes and reliability?

846. Does the schedule include Hybrid Solutions project management time and change request analysis time?

847. What are the duties of the change control team?

848. How do you get changes (code) out in a timely manner?

849. Are change requests logged and managed?

3.3 Change Log: Hybrid Solutions

850. Is the submitted change a new change or a modification of a previously approved change?

851. Is this a mandatory replacement?

852. How does this change affect scope?

853. Is the requested change request a result of changes in other Hybrid Solutions project(s)?

854. Is the change backward compatible without limitations?

855. Will the Hybrid Solutions project fail if the change request is not executed?

856. Is the change request within Hybrid Solutions project scope?

857. Does the suggested change request represent a desired enhancement to the products functionality?

858. When was the request approved?

859. When was the request submitted?

860. Do the described changes impact on the integrity or security of the system?

861. How does this relate to the standards developed for specific business processes?

862. How does this change affect the timeline of the schedule?

863. Where do changes come from?

864. Is the change request open, closed or pending?

865. Who initiated the change request?

3.4 Decision Log: Hybrid Solutions

866. Decision-making process; how will the team make decisions?

867. Who will be given a copy of this document and where will it be kept?

868. What is your overall strategy for quality control / quality assurance procedures?

869. At what point in time does loss become unacceptable?

870. Behaviors; what are guidelines that the team has identified that will assist them with getting the most out of team meetings?

871. With whom was the decision shared or considered?

872. What is the line where eDiscovery ends and document review begins?

873. What are the cost implications?

874. How effective is maintaining the log at facilitating organizational learning?

875. Is everything working as expected?

876. What alternatives/risks were considered?

877. What is the average size of your matters in an

applicable measurement?

878. Which variables make a critical difference?

879. What makes you different or better than others companies selling the same thing?

880. How consolidated and comprehensive a story can you tell by capturing currently available incident data in a central location and through a log of key decisions during an incident?

881. What eDiscovery problem or issue did your organization set out to fix or make better?

882. Meeting purpose; why does this team meet?

883. Is your opponent open to a non-traditional workflow, or will it likely challenge anything you do?

884. How do you define success?

885. How do you know when you are achieving it?

3.5 Quality Audit: Hybrid Solutions

886. How does your organization know that its system for commercializing research outputs is appropriately effective and constructive?

887. Are adequate and conveniently located toilet facilities available for use by the employees?

888. How does your organization know that its quality of teaching is appropriately effective and constructive?

889. Are people allowed to contribute ideas?

890. How does your organization know that its research programs are appropriately effective and constructive?

891. How does your organization know that its staff have appropriate access to a fair and effective grievance process?

892. What is the collective experience of the team to be assigned to an audit?

893. How does your organization know that it provides a safe and healthy environment?

894. Can your organization demonstrate exactly how and why results were achieved?

895. How does the organization know that its system for maintaining and advancing the capabilities of

its staff, particularly in relation to the Mission of the organization, is appropriately effective and constructive?

896. How does your organization know that its information technology system is serving its needs as effectively and constructively as is appropriate?

897. How do you indicate the extent to which your personnel would be expected to contribute to the work effort?

898. Does the audit organization have experience in performing the required work for entities of your type and size?

899. Does the suppliers quality system have a written procedure for corrective action when a defect occurs?

900. How does your organization know that its staff financial services are appropriately effective and constructive?

901. How does your organization know that its Strategic Plan is providing the best guidance for the future of your organization?

902. Are there appropriate means for intervening if necessary?

903. How does your organization know that its staff embody the core knowledge, skills and characteristics for which it wishes to be recognized?

904. How do staff know if they are doing a good job?

905. Are the review comments incorporated?

3.6 Team Directory: Hybrid Solutions

906. Process decisions: which organizational elements and which individuals will be assigned management functions?

907. Who should receive information (all stakeholders)?

908. What needs to be communicated?

909. Who will be the stakeholders on your next Hybrid Solutions project?

910. Process decisions: do invoice amounts match accepted work in place?

911. How will the team handle changes?

912. Decisions: is the most suitable form of contract being used?

913. Who are your stakeholders (customers, sponsors, end users, team members)?

914. When will you produce deliverables?

915. Why is the work necessary?

916. Contract requirements complied with?

917. Where will the product be used and/or delivered or built when appropriate?

918. Process decisions: how well was task order work performed?

919. Process decisions: are there any statutory or regulatory issues relevant to the timely execution of work?

920. Do purchase specifications and configurations match requirements?

921. Have you decided when to celebrate the Hybrid Solutions projects completion date?

922. Process decisions: do job conditions warrant additional actions to collect job information and document on-site activity?

923. Process decisions: is work progressing on schedule and per contract requirements?

924. Who will report Hybrid Solutions project status to all stakeholders?

3.7 Team Operating Agreement: Hybrid Solutions

925. Have you established procedures that team members can follow to work effectively together, such as a team operating agreement?

926. Methodologies: how will key team processes be implemented, such as training, research, work deliverable production, review and approval processes, knowledge management, and meeting procedures?

927. What resources can be provided for the team in terms of equipment, space, time for training, protected time and space for meetings, and travel allowances?

928. How does teaming fit in with overall organizational goals and meet organizational needs?

929. Do you use a parking lot for any items that are important and outside of the agenda?

930. Why does your organization want to participate in teaming?

931. Do you upload presentation materials in advance and test the technology?

932. What is teaming?

933. Do you vary your voice pace, tone and pitch to

engage participants and gain involvement?

934. Are there the right people on your team?

935. Conflict resolution: how will disputes and other conflicts be mediated or resolved?

936. Do you determine the meeting length and time of day?

937. Did you recap the meeting purpose, time, and expectations?

938. How do you want to be thought of and known within your organization?

939. Resource allocation: how will individual team members account for time and expenses, and how will this be allocated in the team budget?

940. What is a Virtual Team?

941. What is culture?

942. Confidentiality: how will confidential information be handled?

943. Must your members collaborate successfully to complete Hybrid Solutions projects?

3.8 Team Performance Assessment: Hybrid Solutions

944. To what degree do the goals specify concrete team work products?

945. To what degree will team members, individually and collectively, commit time to help themselves and others learn and develop skills?

946. To what degree can the team ensure that all members are individually and jointly accountable for the teams purpose, goals, approach, and work-products?

947. Where to from here?

948. Does more radicalness mean more perceived benefits?

949. To what degree do team members articulate the teams work approach?

950. To what degree can the team measure progress against specific goals?

951. How do you manage human resources?

952. Do you give group members authority to make at least some important decisions?

953. To what degree do team members feel that the purpose of the team is important, if not exciting?

954. What is method variance?

955. What structural changes have you made or are you preparing to make?

956. To what degree do team members agree with the goals, relative importance, and the ways in which achievement will be measured?

957. To what degree will new and supplemental skills be introduced as the need is recognized?

958. When does the medium matter?

959. To what degree does the teams purpose contain themes that are particularly meaningful and memorable?

960. To what degree do team members frequently explore the teams purpose and its implications?

961. To what degree can all members engage in open and interactive considerations?

962. How do you keep key people outside the group informed about its accomplishments?

963. To what degree is there a sense that only the team can succeed?

3.9 Team Member Performance Assessment: Hybrid Solutions

964. What is the large, desired outcome?

965. Verify business objectives. Are they appropriate, and well-articulated?

966. To what degree do team members understand one anothers roles and skills?

967. Who should attend?

968. What changes do you need to make to align practices with beliefs?

969. Are any governance changes sufficient to impact achievement?

970. Does adaptive training work?

971. What are top priorities?

972. How are training activities developed from a technical perspective?

973. How are evaluation results utilized?

974. Is it critical or vital to the job?

975. Does the rater (supervisor) have the authority or responsibility to tell an employee that the employees performance is unsatisfactory?

976. Are any validation activities performed?

977. To what degree are the teams goals and objectives clear, simple, and measurable?

978. How do you implement Cost Reduction?

979. To what degree does the teams approach to its work allow for modification and improvement over time?

980. Does the rater (supervisor) have to wait for the interim or final performance assessment review to tell an employee that the employees performance is unsatisfactory?

981. How do you work together to improve teaching and learning?

3.10 Issue Log: Hybrid Solutions

982. Who needs to know and how much?

983. In classifying stakeholders, which approach to do so are you using?

984. Are the Hybrid Solutions project issues uniquely identified, including to which product they refer?

985. How were past initiatives successful?

986. Is the issue log kept in a safe place?

987. What are the stakeholders interrelationships?

988. What is the stakeholders level of authority?

989. Where do team members get information?

990. Who is the issue assigned to?

991. Why multiple evaluators?

992. Which team member will work with each stakeholder?

993. What steps can you take for positive relationships?

994. Do you have members of your team responsible for certain stakeholders?

995. Are there too many who have an interest in some

aspect of your work?

996. Do you feel a register helps?

997. Who are the members of the governing body?

998. What help do you and your team need from the stakeholders?

999. What are the typical contents?

4.0 Monitoring and Controlling Process Group: Hybrid Solutions

1000. How well did you do?

1001. Were sponsors and decision makers available when needed outside regularly scheduled meetings?

1002. Is the program making progress in helping to achieve the set results?

1003. Use: how will they use the information?

1004. What resources are necessary?

1005. Purpose: toward what end is the evaluation being conducted?

1006. Is there adequate validation on required fields?

1007. Propriety: who needs to be involved in the evaluation to be ethical?

1008. Are there areas that need improvement?

1009. What input will you be required to provide the Hybrid Solutions project team?

1010. Is there undesirable impact on staff or resources?

1011. How will staff learn how to use the deliverables?

1012. Where is the Risk in the Hybrid Solutions project?

1013. Change, where should you look for problems?

1014. Does the solution fit in with organizations technical architectural requirements?

1015. Mitigate. what will you do to minimize the impact should a risk event occur?

1016. In what way has the program come up with innovative measures for problem-solving?

1017. Did it work?

1018. What communication items need improvement?

4.1 Project Performance Report: Hybrid Solutions

1019. To what degree can team members meet frequently enough to accomplish the teams ends?

1020. To what degree will the team ensure that all members equitably share the work essential to the success of the team?

1021. To what degree can team members vigorously define the teams purpose in considerations with others who are not part of the functioning team?

1022. To what degree are the goals realistic?

1023. To what degree do all members feel responsible for all agreed-upon measures?

1024. To what degree does the team possess adequate membership to achieve its ends?

1025. To what degree are the structures of the formal organization consistent with the behaviors in the informal organization?

1026. What is the degree to which rules govern information exchange between groups?

1027. To what degree are the demands of the task compatible with and converge with the mission and functions of the formal organization?

1028. To what degree do the structures of the formal organization motivate taskrelevant behavior and facilitate task completion?

1029. To what degree are the goals ambitious?

1030. How can Hybrid Solutions project sustainability be maintained?

1031. How is the data used?

1032. To what degree can the cognitive capacity of individuals accommodate the flow of information?

4.2 Variance Analysis: Hybrid Solutions

1033. Are records maintained to show how management reserves are used?

1034. What does a favorable labor efficiency variance mean?

1035. What is the performance to date and material commitment?

1036. Favorable or unfavorable variance?

1037. Are the bases and rates for allocating costs from each indirect pool consistently applied?

1038. How do you identify potential or actual overruns and underruns?

1039. How do you evaluate the impact of schedule changes, work around, et?

1040. Are significant decision points, constraints, and interfaces identified as key milestones?

1041. What business event caused the fluctuation?

1042. What are the direct labor dollars and/or hours?

1043. Are the requirements for all items of overhead established by rational, traceable processes?

1044. What is exceptional?

1045. Are all cwbs elements specified for external reporting?

1046. Did an existing competitor change strategy?

1047. Is the market likely to continue to grow at this rate next year?

1048. Budgeted cost for work performed?

1049. Other relevant issues of Variance Analysis -selling price or gross margin?

1050. What is the dollar amount of the fluctuation?

1051. How do you identify and isolate causes of favorable and unfavorable cost and schedule variances?

4.3 Earned Value Status: Hybrid Solutions

1052. Where is evidence-based earned value in your organization reported?

1053. Earned value can be used in almost any Hybrid Solutions project situation and in almost any Hybrid Solutions project environment. it may be used on large Hybrid Solutions projects, medium sized Hybrid Solutions projects, tiny Hybrid Solutions projects (in cut-down form), complex and simple Hybrid Solutions projects and in any market sector. some people, of course, know all about earned value, they have used it for years - but perhaps not as effectively as they could have?

1054. What is the unit of forecast value?

1055. How much is it going to cost by the finish?

1056. Are you hitting your Hybrid Solutions projects targets?

1057. Where are your problem areas?

1058. Verification is a process of ensuring that the developed system satisfies the stakeholders agreements and specifications; Are you building the product right? What do you verify?

1059. Validation is a process of ensuring that the developed system will actually achieve the stakeholders desired outcomes; Are you building the right product? What do you validate?

1060. If earned value management (EVM) is so good in determining the true status of a Hybrid Solutions project and Hybrid Solutions project its completion, why is it that hardly any one uses it in information systems related Hybrid Solutions projects?

1061. When is it going to finish?

1062. How does this compare with other Hybrid Solutions projects?

4.4 Risk Audit: Hybrid Solutions

1063. Does your auditor understand your business?

1064. What are risks and how do you manage them?

1065. What limitations do auditors face in effectively applying risk-assessment results to the risk of material misstatement measures?

1066. Is there (or should there be) some impact on the process of setting materiality when the auditor more effectively identifies higher risk areas of the financial statements?

1067. Is the customer technically sophisticated in the product area?

1068. Extending the consideration on the halo effect, to what extent are auditors able to build skepticism in evidence review?

1069. Are requirements fully understood by the team and customers?

1070. Do you have position descriptions for all key paid and volunteer positions in your organization?

1071. Is all expenditure authorised through an identified process?

1072. Have staff received necessary training?

1073. Is there a screening process that will ensure all

participants have the fitness and skills required to safely participate?

1074. Do you meet all obligations relating to funds secured from grants, loans and sponsors?

1075. Have top software and customer managers formally committed to support the Hybrid Solutions project?

1076. Who is responsible for what?

1077. Has everyone (staff, volunteers and participants) agreed to a code of behaviour or conduct?

1078. For paid staff, does your organization comply with the minimum conditions for employment and/or the applicable modern award?

1079. Have all possible risks/hazards been identified (including injury to staff, damage to equipment, impact on others in the community)?

1080. Have risks been considered with an insurance broker or provider and suitable insurance cover been arranged?

1081. What does monitoring consist of?

4.5 Contractor Status Report: Hybrid Solutions

1082. Who can list a Hybrid Solutions project as organization experience, your organization or a previous employee of your organization?

1083. What was the final actual cost?

1084. Describe how often regular updates are made to the proposed solution. Are corresponding regular updates included in the standard maintenance plan?

1085. What was the actual budget or estimated cost for your organizations services?

1086. How does the proposed individual meet each requirement?

1087. What process manages the contracts?

1088. How is risk transferred?

1089. What are the minimum and optimal bandwidth requirements for the proposed solution?

1090. How long have you been using the services?

1091. If applicable; describe your standard schedule for new software version releases. Are new software version releases included in the standard maintenance plan?

1092. What is the average response time for answering a support call?

1093. What was the overall budget or estimated cost?

1094. What was the budget or estimated cost for your organizations services?

1095. Are there contractual transfer concerns?

4.6 Formal Acceptance: Hybrid Solutions

1096. Was the Hybrid Solutions project goal achieved?

1097. Was business value realized?

1098. Is formal acceptance of the Hybrid Solutions project product documented and distributed?

1099. Do you buy pre-configured systems or build your own configuration?

1100. Does it do what Hybrid Solutions project team said it would?

1101. Did the Hybrid Solutions project achieve its MOV?

1102. Was the Hybrid Solutions project work done on time, within budget, and according to specification?

1103. Who would use it?

1104. Was the client satisfied with the Hybrid Solutions project results?

1105. Do you buy-in installation services?

1106. Do you perform formal acceptance or burn-in tests?

1107. How does your team plan to obtain formal

acceptance on your Hybrid Solutions project?

1108. What are the requirements against which to test, Who will execute?

1109. What lessons were learned about your Hybrid Solutions project management methodology?

1110. Have all comments been addressed?

1111. Does it do what client said it would?

1112. What features, practices, and processes proved to be strengths or weaknesses?

1113. What can you do better next time?

1114. General estimate of the costs and times to complete the Hybrid Solutions project?

1115. Was the Hybrid Solutions project managed well?

5.0 Closing Process Group: Hybrid Solutions

1116. What will you do to minimize the impact should a risk event occur?

1117. Based on your Hybrid Solutions project communication management plan, what worked well?

1118. Was the user/client satisfied with the end product?

1119. What is the risk of failure to your organization?

1120. Is this an updated Hybrid Solutions project Proposal Document?

1121. Did the delivered product meet the specified requirements and goals of the Hybrid Solutions project?

1122. What is the overall risk of the Hybrid Solutions project to your organization?

1123. What could be done to improve the process?

1124. Is the Hybrid Solutions project funded?

1125. Can the lesson learned be replicated?

1126. How well did the team follow the chosen processes?

1127. Is there a clear cause and effect between the activity and the lesson learned?

1128. How well did the chosen processes fit the needs of the Hybrid Solutions project?

1129. What could have been improved?

1130. What were the actual outcomes?

5.1 Procurement Audit: Hybrid Solutions

1131. Were results of the award procedures published?

1132. If the expert was allowed to submit a tender, was all the relevant information the expert had gained from his earlier involvement made available to the other bidders?

1133. When negotiation took place in successive stages, was this practice stated in the procurement documents and was it done in accordance with the award criteria stated?

1134. Are there mechanisms in place to evaluate the performance of the departments suppliers?

1135. Are budget transfers within the general fund made for only the already stated items permitted by law and regulation?

1136. Was confidentiality ensured when necessary?

1137. If information was withheld, was there reasonable justification for this decision?

1138. Is there any objection?

1139. Are the internal control systems operational?

1140. Does the department have a procurement

strategy and is it implemented?

1141. Did the bidder comply with requests within the deadline set?

1142. Does the procurement process compile basic procurement information such as how much is bought and spend with individual suppliers?

1143. Is free and fair (international) competition promoted by organizational policies and legislation, in line with legal, trade organizations and other policies?

1144. Is there no evidence that the consultants participating in the Hybrid Solutions project design released information to contractors competing for the prime contract?

1145. Are information technology resources (e-procurement) used to reduce costs?

1146. If a purchase order calls for a cost-plus agreement, is the method of determining how final charges will be determined specified?

1147. Audits: when was your last independent public accountant (ipa) audit and what were the results?

1148. Are risks managed to provide reasonable assurance regarding department procurement objectives?

1149. Did additional works amount to no more than 50% of the initial contract?

1150. Are staff members evaluated in accordance with the terms of existing negotiated agreements?

5.2 Contract Close-Out: Hybrid Solutions

1151. Have all contracts been completed?

1152. What happens to the recipient of services?

1153. Have all acceptance criteria been met prior to final payment to contractors?

1154. Have all contract records been included in the Hybrid Solutions project archives?

1155. What is capture management?

1156. Parties: Authorized?

1157. Have all contracts been closed?

1158. Was the contract complete without requiring numerous changes and revisions?

1159. Change in attitude or behavior?

1160. How does it work?

1161. How/when used ?

1162. Parties: who is involved?

1163. Are the signers the authorized officials?

1164. Change in knowledge?

1165. How is the contracting office notified of the automatic contract close-out?

1166. Was the contract sufficiently clear so as not to result in numerous disputes and misunderstandings?

1167. Change in circumstances?

1168. Has each contract been audited to verify acceptance and delivery?

1169. Was the contract type appropriate?

5.3 Project or Phase Close-Out: Hybrid Solutions

1170. What stakeholder group needs, expectations, and interests are being met by the Hybrid Solutions project?

1171. Is the lesson based on actual Hybrid Solutions project experience rather than on independent research?

1172. What are the informational communication needs for each stakeholder?

1173. What was the preferred delivery mechanism?

1174. What hierarchical authority does the stakeholder have in your organization?

1175. Complete yes or no?

1176. Were cost budgets met?

1177. What are the marketing communication needs for each stakeholder?

1178. What was expected from each stakeholder?

1179. Have business partners been involved extensively, and what data was required for them?

1180. What benefits or impacts does the stakeholder group expect to obtain as a result of the Hybrid

Solutions project?

1181. What is a Risk Management Process?

1182. What is a Risk?

1183. When and how were information needs best met?

1184. Planned completion date?

1185. How often did each stakeholder need an update?

1186. What can you do better next time, and what specific actions can you take to improve?

5.4 Lessons Learned: Hybrid Solutions

1187. Was sufficient advance training conducted and/or information provided to enable the already stated affected by the changes to adjust to and accommodate them?

1188. What were the success factors?

1189. How effective were your functional specs?

1190. How much time is required for the task?

1191. What is your organizational ideology?

1192. How accurately and timely was the Risk Management Log updated or reviewed?

1193. How effective were Hybrid Solutions project audits?

1194. How effective were the communications materials in providing and orienting team members about the details of the Hybrid Solutions project?

1195. How useful and complete was the Hybrid Solutions project document repository?

1196. How well was Hybrid Solutions project status communicated throughout your involvement in the Hybrid Solutions project?

1197. What are the internal dependencies?

1198. What solutions or recommendations can you offer that would have improved some aspect of the Hybrid Solutions project?

1199. How well were your expectations met regarding the extent of your involvement in the Hybrid Solutions project (effort, time commitments, etc.)?

1200. What is your overall assessment of the outcome of this Hybrid Solutions project?

1201. What Hybrid Solutions project circumstances were not anticipated?

1202. What is below the surface?

1203. Is your organization willing to expose problems or mistakes for the betterment of the collective whole, and can you do this in a way that does not intimidate employees or workers?

1204. What is the supervisor to staff ratio?

Index

control 2, 30, 53, 88, 92-95, 97-98, 130, 135, 150-151, 153, 166, 174, 177, 217-218, 221, 252
controlled   70, 173
controls   18, 64, 67, 75, 79, 86, 90-91, 94, 97, 160, 203
convention   114
converge   238
conversion   146
convey   1
convince   188, 192
cooperate   177
Copyright   1
correct 43, 88, 135, 181
corrective   48, 96, 224
correspond   8-9
costing 44, 151, 176
cost-plus   253
counsel   208
counting   155
course 32, 55, 242
covering   8, 95
coworker   120
crashing   160
craziest   101
create 21, 59, 105, 119, 218
created   66, 95, 129, 133-134, 152, 174
creating   7, 52, 137, 147
creation   200
creative   16
creativity   81
credible   177
crisis   19
criteria 2, 5, 8-9, 34-35, 71, 76, 80, 97, 104, 111, 124, 140, 142, 178, 207-208, 252, 255
CRITERION   2, 15, 27, 43, 57, 73, 88, 100
critical 28-29, 66, 82, 90, 99, 126, 146, 155, 205, 207, 222, 232
Crosby 166
cross-sell   103
crucial 58, 130
crystal 10
culture 37, 60, 189-191, 229
cumbersome   196
current 42-45, 60, 63, 72, 79, 96, 111-113, 118, 146-147, 160, 181, 185, 187, 191, 209, 214

proved 249

provide 19, 64, 115-116, 118, 129, 151, 160, 169, 177, 184, 236, 253

provided 11, 96, 166-167, 181, 192, 205, 207, 228, 259

provider 245

providers 83

provides 159, 223

providing 96, 129, 145, 224, 259

public 253

published 205, 208, 252

publisher 1

pulled 101

purchase 7, 208, 227, 253

purchased 150

purpose 2, 9, 121, 127, 144, 164-165, 177, 222, 229-231, 236, 238

purposes 127

pushing 110

qualified 30, 57, 63, 67-69, 134, 191

qualifies 64, 68

qualify 52, 65, 71

qualities 23

quality 1, 4-5, 9, 16, 47, 54, 60, 63-64, 69, 94-95, 126, 132, 136-137, 153, 166, 173, 181, 183, 185-186, 189-192, 205, 213, 221, 223-224

quantified 89

quantify 52

question 10, 15, 27, 43, 57, 73, 88, 100, 103, 195

questions 7-8, 10, 61, 139

quickly 9, 65, 68, 70, 195

radically 67

ranking 201

rather 117, 257

rating 207

rational 240

reached 16

reaching 112

readiness 28, 152

readings 91

realistic 16, 70, 109, 134, 172, 199, 238

reality 179

realize 48

realized 116, 248

CPSIA information can be obtained
at www.ICGtesting.com
Printed in the USA
BVHW041011200819

556236BV00011B/723/P

9 780655 843009